THE LOG HOME BOOK

DESIGN, PAST & PRESENT

CINDY TEIPNER-THIEDE AND ARTHUR THIEDE

PHOTOGRAPHY BY JONATHAN STOKE AND CINDY TEIPNER-THIEDE

GIBBS-SMITH
P
PUBLISHER

SALT LAKE CITY

97   5

This is a Peregrine Smith Book, published by
Gibbs Smith, Publisher
P.O. Box 667
Layton, Utah 84041

Printed in Hong Kong

Design by Leesha Gibby Jones
Lynda Sessions, Editor
Dawn Valentine Hadlock, Editorial Assistant

Library of Congress Cataloging-in-Publication Data
Thiede, Cindy Teipner, 1958–
        The log home book / Arthur Thiede.
               p.   cm.
        Includes bibliographical references and index.
        ISBN 0–87905–671–1 (pbk.)
        1. Log cabins—United States. I. Thiede, Arthur. II. Title.
NA8470.T49   1993
728' .37' 0973—dc20

                                                        93—14069
                                                        CIP

TABLE OF CONTENTS

ACKNOWLEDGEMENTS

When we set out to write our second book on log home architecture, our lives weren't quite as simple as they were in 1983 when everything we owned, including camera equipment, fit into the back of our 1972 Dodge van. This time around we had our own log home, two small boys, and a thriving business. As a result, Art had to stay home and hold down the fort, while photographer jonathan stoke of Heliographs Photography in Hailey, Idaho and I did a whirlwind tour of the country to photograph the houses for this book. We are especially grateful to jonathan for his patience, perseverance and professionalism, in spite of long hours, leaky tents and the inevitable auto mishaps.

By the same token, both jonathan and I wish to thank the many friends and acquaintances along the way who extended their homes and hospitality to us. Thanks to James Morton; Al and Deeann Baldwin; Mike and Laura Neary; Gerry and Imaging Spence; Richard Lewis; the Beadlestons; Ellie and Harry Fox; Betty and David Kolosta; Richard Tuxbury, Jeff Knebl and Maple Island Log Homes; Charles and Linda McRaven and their delightful children; Quebec, Canada's, fabulous Le Chateau Montebello; The staff at the Sagamore Institute in Raquette Lake, New York; Ken and Sherrie Jern of The Wildflower Inn in Jackson Hole, Wyoming—a superb bed and breakfast; Crosby Brown and Karen LaBoube; and Barry and Darlene Gregson.

Heartfelt thanks also go to my sister-in-law Sonya Perler and to my dear friends Cary Jones; Sue and Todd Cedarholm; Ellen Schaefer; and Bill Howard and Pat Bishop who generously permitted us to intrude on their busy lives, while adding both warmth and intrigue to our visit. Thank you also, Heather Mehra, a personal confidante whose support and last minute editing skills helped us carry this book to print. Praise also to Mary Jones, a friend and local artist who recast our log home in gingerbread for a Christmas picture I wish we could have used.

In the course of our travels, we photographed the fabulous homes pictured here, as well as several others that could not be featured because of space limitations. Our editorial choices were not easy ones, and we are indebted to each and every home owner, architect, designer and builder who helped us in our quest.

Our appreciation also goes out to the entire staff at F-Stop Camera & Video in Ketchum, Idaho, and particularly to Jack Flolo, Wade Burwell and Danette Straub who processed our film promptly and professionally. Fritz Bjornsen and Mark Wildman of the Darkroom in Boise, Idaho, did an equally fine job with our large format, black and white film.

In researching this book, we relied heavily on the resources of individual builders and log home companies in the United States and Canada. We are grateful to them all. Richard Bray of Ex Libris bookstore in Sun Valley, Idaho, also graciously permitted us to use his store like a library—allowing us access to the most up-to-date home source books available.

Finally, I would personally like to acknowledge my family. I am so grateful to my husband Art, who as co-author of this book, also endured the added challenge of single parenting while I was away. As for my beautiful boys, Tyler and Jesse, I want to sneak in a simple "I love you."

DEDICATION

On April 25, 1992, Francis Lee Smith was killed in a fall while working on his home outside of Cody, Wyoming. His death brought an end to his dreams and to eighteen years of strenuous labor. To his memory we dedicate this book.

It was in the summer of 1984 when we saw "it." We were heading east from Yellowstone Park towards Cody, Wyoming, having driven through spectacular countryside for the past several hours. At first we thought our eyes were playing tricks on us. From a distance the structure looked like some throwback to early mining days. As we drove closer, we saw that it was partially built with logs. With our interest piqued further, we detoured up a rocky dirt road to find Lee Smith, hard at work. In our ensuing conversations, we became fascinated with both Lee and his dream.

Using recycled materials, Lee had already been working some ten years on his home and, by his own calculations, had at least ten more to go. Everything from foundation excavation to horse logging was done without the use of heavy machinery. Even the beams, logs, rafters and trusses were lifted onto the structure by hand. Fast becoming his life's work, Lee was totally consumed by his project—a monument to the mountains he explored and loved so much.

While the structure is impressive, we also marvel that Lee built his home while maintaining a full-time job in Cody as an engineer. Working through eighteen years of weekends, vacations, and late nights, his perseverance was as formidable as the building itself.

You have built your castle Lee, now rest in peace.

PREFACE

Because whole logs presented a simple and complete building material to those who lived in their midst, they were used abundantly for early shelter by a variety of people around the world. As need, desire and technology furthered impatient cultures along, log home construction faded in and out of popularity. However, with its roots ground firmly in tradition, log home living became a guarded component of the cultural heritage of many countries.

Perhaps nowhere is this more apropos than in America—a country bound by tradition yet dominated by diversity and change. Here unfettered creative energy gives rise to an endless array of trends, technologies and fashions. While many are no more than fads, others develop and mature with age. America's affiliation with log homes is one enduring example.

In 1986 when we published our first book, *American Log Homes,* we noted that log home building had come of age. We documented the rise of logs from humble shelters on the frontier to a multi-million dollar industry. *American Log Homes* opened doors for many would-be owners, builders, architects and designers who previously had been limited by misconceptions or stereotypes. Over the years, feedback from inspired readers has left us with a strong feeling of accomplishment, as well as with the recognition that our work had only just begun.

Today, the industry continues to surge ahead both here and abroad—expanding, experimenting and fine-tuning as it goes. Within North America, western styles of building are moving east and eastern styles are going west. In countries like Japan and Russia, inspired woodworkers are reawakening the age old art. Everywhere architects and builders continue to revolutionize their designs via creative mixing and matching of various building materials. Options for finishing, detailing and decorating log homes are virtually limitless, and innovative approaches to staining and painting add yet another dimension.

All this adds up to a wealth of new ideas for the architect, builder, interior designer and buyer of today's log homes. Yet all is not new with logs, and there is another fascination with the tree and its ancient history that attracts us. Unlike many other forms of contemporary architecture, logs represent a closeness to the earth that we can see and touch. For all their newfound versatility, logs retain an emotional advantage that continues to endear them to us in our highly technological world.

Having said that, *The Log Home Book* is about the old and the new—the old because it is about the lessons of our architectural past, the new because it is full of novel ideas and fresh approaches to designing, building and decorating our lasting legacy of wooden houses.

▲ *The only windmill in the valley is more than a conversation piece for the Thiedes. It adds to the farmstead character they have tried to develop on the property.*

INTRODUCTION

It was in the spring of 1987 when the realtor's words stung in my ears. "Congratulations! The lot is yours."

Congratulations? I hated that lot—two and one-half acres of high desert scruff—flat as a pancake and bordered to the east by a noisy, overburdened highway. A tangled mess of chokecherry bushes and aging cottonwoods provided some relief along the roadside, but they were dying of thirst and sure to be a hazard of some sort.

The lot was in the Wood River Valley just ten miles south of Idaho's famous Sun Valley ski resort. We'd been here for nearly ten years and didn't want for beauty — it was all around us. I just didn't see it right then, at least not between the corner posts of this scrappy lot that we had somehow just acquired.

Art, my husband, was ecstatic. He'd figured we'd just gotten a great deal on a dreamable piece of property, and while I sat worrying about how we'd keep our first born son from someday toddling into the oncoming path of a Mack truck, Art spent hours pacing through his thorn-infested plot envisioning our home.

There was no question that we would build with logs. After all, we wrote the book on it — at least we wrote one book called *American Log Homes*. Besides, Art had earned his living as a log builder for over a decade, and we were beginning to doubt our own credibility — not ever having actually lived in a log house! Here, finally, was our chance to live out the experiences we had previously only borrowed from so many others.

It's just that highway noise and sticker bushes hadn't been programmed into my log house dream scene. In fact, as I think about it, my dream scene was rather vague. We had travelled the country photographing hundreds of beautiful homes. We had seen everything from the frontier traditional to fanatical nouveau. There had been homes in the mountains and homes at the seaside, and though I can't quite remember, there must have been at least one log home in the sticker bushes. Now everything was

getting all mixed up on the canvas in my mind.

People often commented that our own log house must truly be a marvel — having seen so many, they assumed ours would be some kind of exotic architectural wonder — or at least it should be. Perhaps, I was feeling the same way. In fact, shouldn't our lot be secluded among tall pines, complete with babbling brook, earthshaking views, and a herd of deer all our own? Well, surely babbling brooks wouldn't come cheap, and we were on a strict budget. Anyway, we already had the lot.

I think it was Wednesday when I loaded up our baby son, Tyler and drove over to reassess our new home site. Art was already there, tape measure in one hand, pad in the other and a pencil stuck behind his ear. Tyler was sleeping in his car seat, and I didn't wake him as I stepped out into our field. Before I knew it I was knee deep in sage — not so brittle as I had remembered and slightly fragrant with the first blooms of spring. I stood in the middle of those two and one-half acres with my back to the highway. The sky was blue and the air remarkably fresh. I looked past the western edge of our property, past the neighbor's barn, the greening pasture and budding groves of aspen trees. There were still small patches of snow clinging to the shadows of the valley wall that rose abruptly from the banks of the Big Wood River flowing not more than a quarter-mile away. To the north, the mountains, though more distant, prevailed with dignity on the landscape. To the south, the sky overtook the mountains as they tumbled out of the valley's mouth.

I walked full circle around the lot, noting new life in the scribbled maze of bush and tree along the highway. Then I saw something else that jolted my subconscious— a simple nest, probably a robin's, not more than six feet off the ground. It was tightly woven and looked as if it had been made that very year. I pushed my way through the tangle to get a closer look. Though not more than thirty feet from the road, it was totally concealed. That nest is safe, I thought, embraced by its own little world within a world. Then, knowing that the chicks would hatch and grow to flight that spring, I begin to see our lot and future home in a whole new way.

For the first time, it occurred to me that, in my mind, I had been building someone else's house in some other place. It was someone else's sense of beauty that I'd been trying to second guess—someone else who I'd been trying to impress. Like that robin, we would create our own little world. Our house would not be some architectural wonder, but it would be secure, environmentally compatible and functionally beautiful. Yes, we would draw from our great basin of knowledge filled in the course of travel and experience, but we would be selective in the concepts we applied.

By Saturday, we had a plan. This would not be just a house, but a homestead. The main house would be built near the front of the property and as far from the road as possible. Our log barn would go up behind the house to wall out the frenzy of highway commuters and overamped tourists. To the south, between the house and barn would be a third building combining a shop and guest apartment for Art's elderly father. Short berms would be built up between the barn, shop and main house. In effect, the three buildings would create the feel of a large courtyard. With the gift of water, we vowed that our roadside vegetation would not perish, and dozens of other trees and bushes would be planted where they might best appease the senses. The pasture behind the barn would be irrigated and a windmill would be poised for pumping water. There would even be a few rusty farm implements and an old truck strategically placed so as not to raise the ire of our completely tidy homeowners association.

The front of the house would face westward, drinking in those views I'd so recently discovered, and a glorious little sun room would be added on the south. The overall design of each log building would be simple, affordable and functional. Art and his small crew would

hand peel every log on site then weave each trunk into the sturdy fabric of our walls. In the weeks that followed, that small bird's nest came to mind more than once.

That spring and summer, we watched our house grow up from the earth while the world around turned green. The freshly peeled logs sparkled in the sun and beckoned to be touched. The scent of pine permeated the air. There was life in those log walls, and their very presence gave heart to the land around them.

One year later, we had made that house our home. Two years later, Art put the finishing touches on the barn, and three years later, our young trees had come into their own. The highway, its roar muted, still raced by somewhere in the distance, and stickers still pressed into my socks as my two young sons and I explored the fringes of our homestead in search of garter snakes. A fox had taken up residence somewhere nearby, a skunk demanded rent-free space beneath our back deck, and the deer harvested my garden with carefree abandon. I grinned shamelessly, and for a brief moment, I imagined we had carved out a wilderness, in the midst of civilization.

So it was that we affirmed log home living for ourselves—and in doing so gained further insight and appreciation for the craft to which we devote this book. Most owner built or designed homes are an extension of their makers. They say something to the world about those living within and their relationship to creation around them. Log homes, by their very nature link us more deeply to a tangible awareness of the earth and our natural environment. This link may seem frail at times, but I have met very few log home owners who have not made some conscious attempt to express this felt or desired connection.

This is not to say that the log homes of today are of a "back to nature" sort. On the contrary, logs offer us a fascinating and remarkably adaptable building material. But there is an undeniable history associated with this craft — one that deepens our connection and begs remembrance of our roots.

The log home experience has known a vividly diverse existence being born and reborn into a multitude of cultures around the world. Originating in Russia, then spreading throughout Scandinavia and northern Europe, the craft endured for centuries before Swedish and Finnish immigrants settled in America in 1638. Introducing their skills anew, these robust individuals inspired the tradition that our nation has come to call her own.

Built under difficult circumstances, most early dwellings were crude and stark—shelters born not so much of choice but of necessity. This very need, however, fueled by courage, rugged determination and pride, rallied early pioneers to inspirit a nation. As such, America and Canada fondly remember the log cabin as the shelter they grew up in. Perhaps it is only fitting that the same dwelling from which we conquered the land now, in some small way, weds us to it.

As decades passed and the frontier expanded beyond forest boundaries, the premise for building with logs gradually changed from one motivated by convenience and necessity to one of desirability. That is, people actually sought out log houses but didn't want, or have, to build them themselves. With enterprising young craftsman eager to oblige, the business of logs came in from the woods.

The advent of "off-site" building in the 1970s, coupled with ample supplies of dead-standing timber and soon thereafter, with the development of synthetic chinking, set the stage for the advancement of an industry that now includes hundreds of manufacturers throughout the United States and Canada.

This ambitious enterprise has not grown through the ranks unchallenged, but in overcoming both real and imagined obstacles in terms of design, decor and energy efficiency, the log home merits more credibility today than ever before.

In *The Log Home Book,* we'll take you down the circuitous path of possibility—examining historical re-creations along with the handiwork of an industry moving in new and different directions. In acknowledging the growth and success of the trade, we pay special attention to the inventive achievements of home decorators and interior designers. While it is one thing to imagine the quintessential room, it may be quite another to produce it. Logs can be a challenging medium to work with—especially for the individual who is intimidated by little inconsistencies such as bumpy walls. Regardless of hurdles, designers have risen to the occasion with inspiring interiors that continue to delight and surprise.

As logs yield to the creative personalities of individual home builders, we are also witness to other exciting innovations in contemporary home design—such as the increasing use of logs for "accent." Today there is a growing movement afoot to combine conventional walls with logs for structure and aesthetics. The popularity of this post-and-beam architecture has grown tremendously in recent years, and while not truly log in the conventional sense, this form of building requires the finely honed skills of experienced craftsmen. As a result, post-and- beam construction has gained a rightful place in the log home industry, and we enthusiastically display it here.

With an open mind and healthy imagination, nearly anything is possible. Yet, while log home ownership can be particularly rewarding, it also brings with it a unique set of design and maintenance considerations. As the architect, builder, or buyer set their dreams to paper, they will need to operate from a base of knowledge on subjects ranging from weatherization and insect control to chinking and wall settling. To acquaint the reader with these topics, we have included a final informational chapter condensed from our own experience and other resources.

There is perhaps nothing more personal than the space in which we live and, at the same time, nothing that reveals so much about us. The temptation to design outside ourselves is always present, but in staying true to our physical and emotional needs we can create beautiful, functional and empowering environments that will enrich our lives. This is not to say that an education is not necessary or that one can disregard essential principles of environment and structure. Rely on the expert to help guide your vision.

Experience and enjoy the successes of others then take hold of that which you admire, and remake it for yourself.

◄ *Cindy and Art Thiede blocked out highway noise and created privacy in back with the creative placement of their house, barn, shop and landscaped berms.*

1 ꝉ EASTERN TRADITIONAL

The East is a beginning place. Where city meets country, a sense of time and change are juxtaposed. The landscape cradles remnants of our historic past, and we can visit the very places where our founding fathers once stood in memorable acts of duty and discovery. It was on eastern shores that America took root, and it was here that the homes of common people first initiated our architectural evolution.

The log cabin rose out of the forests as the logical form of shelter on a spirited frontier. Yet there is a distinction to be made between these cabins and the settlers' more civilized log homes. The cabin, a temporary structure, was built hastily with round logs. Often a by-product of the frenzied westward rush, thousands were chopped recklessly from the woods. Where time and opportunity permitted, however, a more permanent home would be carefully crafted from logs flattened on two sides— hence the hewn-log home. Not only were the resulting smooth walls more familiar and socially acceptable, but with the outer bark and decay-prone sapwood removed, these buildings survived for generations.

In the East and parts of the Midwest, one does not have to travel far from the entrapment of city life to find these vestiges of pioneer culture carefully restored and adapted for contemporary living. These enduring hewn-log homes present a window through time and a way that we can learn from and appreciate our architectural past. The buildings that remain are fine examples of the pioneers' craft, and their designs mirror the honest needs and aesthetic consciousness of the people who first built them.

Because the East came first, so it seems that many of our contemporary trends and innovations should also arise there. It isn't surprising then, after the fabled pioneer cabin gave way to modern convenience and milled lumber in the 1800s, log building should be resurrected again decades later in none other than upstate New York. Under the leadership of William West Durant, the "Adirondack Camp" style emerged in the latter part of the nineteenth century. These distinctive rustic retreats, designed for the wealthy aristocracy of the East, were characterized by the unique application of unpeeled logs, branches, twigs, bark and stone. These self sufficient "camps," each incorporating up to twenty or more carefully designed and handcrafted buildings, were equipped to indulge the most genteel of clients.

The catalyst for this second coming of logs in America was a far cry from the forces driving the nation's struggling first families. The outcome, however, proved no less inspiring to those who would ultimately deliver log homes into the present. The Adirondack era heralded in a new approach to log building where, for the first time, architects stepped in to direct the design and construction of the American log home.

The Past Recycled

Because I was born and raised in the West, I grew up with a different sense of early American history. I never realized just how different that sense was until after college when Art and I travelled to the East to research the manuscript for our first book. What I had read in school was intellectual and distant. What I experienced when we explored Civil War battlefields and the boyhood homes of celebrated presidents was emotional and real. But it wasn't until after I had visited those log homes inspired by romantic notions of a bygone era and built from the salvaged remains of forgotten dwellings that history leaped from its pages and touched my soul.

Some of these old homes, recycled into the twentieth century by highly skilled men and women, were originally built and occupied by families nearly two hundred years ago. Two hundred years! Oh, if only these old logs could speak—but they can and do. There are some highly devoted

▲ *This two-story home built by Charles McRaven is of huge white pine logs. First floor logs, now lighter than those above them, had once been whitewashed, and a porch overhang protected them from weather. Although all the logs have since been cleaned and treated, the telltale signs remain.*

modern-day craftsmen who can read this log house language and deduce the course of events that shaped the lives of early pioneers. The type of nails and screws used, saw marks on logs, door latches and the assembly of the house are just a few ways a building reveals its age and history. Nail holes and pegs, worn stairs and floorings, room additions, gun portals and a hundred other features tell the story of the people who lived there. Knowing which parts of the home are original and what has been added or adapted over the years is an art unto itself.

Lured by the invention and individuality of the past, antiquarians and master builders like Crosby Brown and Charles McRaven have made the discovery and restoration of old hewn-log homes a part of their life's work. Whether recreated in their original form or adapted to suit more contemporary designs, these homes are reborn into the lives of families who will impart new secrets to the logs. The stories they retell two hundred years from now will, no doubt, be quite different.

Historical Restorations Recall Days of Old—The Work of Wheelock "Crosby" Brown

Green Restoration

Crosby Brown is a student of architectural history specializing in historic restorations and trans-Mississippi history. As a resident of eastern Missouri, he began working as the chief of state historical sites in 1965. After supervising state restorations for several years, he left the department to start his own business in 1972. Utilizing geological survey maps of early settlement areas along the Missouri River, Crosby spent many a weekend exploring back roads and knocking on farmers' doors in search of deserted houses. Hidden beneath old clapboard, paneling and plaster, Crosby often found the treasure he sought. Among his cherished finds were four eighteenth century vertical-log homes, several other horizontal-log structures, and, surprisingly, musty rooms filled with highly collectible antiques! Boarded up and abandoned, some of these prizes could be had for a song.

▲ *The log portion of this historic home is built from ancient white oak. Unlike many other salvaged dwellings, these logs had never been covered with clapboard siding. Instead, the ample two-story porches protected the wood from weather, and only a few logs on the gable ends needed replacement.*

Homes still salvageable from decay were thoroughly photographed and meticulously documented before being disassembled and moved to a new location. One such home was first built in 1798 by James Green, a settler who brought his family from New Bern, North Carolina, in 1797 to settle his own land grant in St. Charles County, Missouri.

Of English descent, Green combined the building traditions of his birthright with those of both French and Swedish settlers to create one of the most unusual examples of early American log home architecture still in existence. From the Swedes, he borrowed horizontal hewn-log construction. From French tradition, he incorporated two-story gallery porches in both front and back, and from his own English background, he devised a stone chimney that stepped away from the house between the first and second stories so that cooking fires

◀ Hollowed out and lined with aluminum, cedar pole gutters empty into replicas of early nineteenth century downspouts. Homesteaders didn't usually drink rain water, but it was used regularly for washing.

▼ Sally Brown nurtures a garden of herbs, flowers and vegetables on the site that will one day serve as a foundation for a third historic addition to their house.

in summer wouldn't overheat the upstairs. Not only was it unusual to see such an amalgamation of building styles, but this rare two-story house was also built atop a full basement.

Crosby purchased the Green house in 1968, and despite the fact that it had been lived in continuously until 1961, it was nearly 99 percent original. Neither the outside logs nor inside walls had ever been sided over or covered with plaster. There was still no central heating, plumbing or electricity and all the original interior and exterior woodwork, flooring, glass and sashes were intact.

After making dozens of carefully measured drawings, taking hundreds of photographs and marking every piece of the house down to the last chimney stone, Crosby moved the building to a comparable riverside site just twenty-five miles away. Here, he painstakingly reconstructed the house as a retirement home for his parents, Lyle and Sally Brown. Apart from carefully concealed electrical outlets and a heating system, the house was rebuilt almost exactly as it had been nearly two hundred years ago. To accommodate bathrooms, a kitchen, and interior stairway, an 1830s frame addition was attached. Previously, the only access to the second floor of the Green house was by a stairway located outside under the front porch. There are still more plans in the works to attach yet another historic addition built of stone. Tons of marked rock, from a home erected in 1800, lie ready on the property.

◀ *Crosby Brown searched for more than a year, walking every hill within fifty miles, before finding an historically accurate building site overlooking the Missouri River. The house now stands where the river bends, and views of the water can be enjoyed from both porches.*

▲ *Lyle and Sally's beds now rest against the opposite wall in this second-story room that originally slept the Greens' five children. Unusual features include the chair rails found both upstairs and down. These rails kept furniture from rubbing up against the logs, whereas in conventional construction, it is the walls, not the furniture, that usually need protection! The lookout windows, left and right of the fireplace, came in handy during the War of 1812, when more than six hundred people were killed within fifty miles of the homestead. The blanket crane above the mantle is another rare find in a house west of the Mississippi.*

▶ *The original shutters on this home were missing, but hand-forged hardware and other clues led Crosby to install plank shutters he adapted from those found on an old schoolhouse. Ten years later, when a fellow happened by with a pocket full of house pictures taken in 1923, Crosby was delighted to see that he had guessed right.*

▲ *The living room basks in the patina of period antiques collected by the Browns through more than fifty years of marriage. The fireplace remains a focal point with its original walnut mantle and cooking crane. In earlier days, hot coals burned beneath simmering pots 365 days a year, and at the hearth, more than half of the two-inch-thick hand-hewn, white oak flooring has been worn away by generations of fire tenders.*

◄ *This bathroom, housed in the 1930s addition, is fitted with an old dry sink adapted for running water. Like all other rooms in the house, it is flued for a wood-stove.*

◀ *"Factor" or chief trader Joseph Chardron lived in this one room section of the fort with his Osage Indian wife and two children. Today the room contains all the authentic trappings for life lived on the edge of the extreme frontier.*

▼ *This rare eighteenth century watercolor of a French trans-Mississippi fur trader is displayed on the fort wall with a highly prized collection of personal possessions that includes crosses, a trade medal, snuff horn, and bait pouch.*

Fort Charrette

Just down the road from the Brown house, Crosby brings trans-Mississippi history to life again in his restoration of Fort Charrette. This salty old trading post, built in 1790 just nine miles from its present location, was operated by Joseph Chardron until 1803. Chardron, chief trader, or "factor" as he was commonly called, exchanged store bought goods from St. Louis for furs from native Osage and Missouri Indians.

Charrette is the French word for "little cart." It was in this small two-wheeled wagon that they hauled furs and trading supplies to and from the Missouri River for transport. The fort consists of three main rooms plus a giant loft. The trading post, a central work area and the chief trader's living quarters were housed downstairs while cleaned and salted furs were stored above. Through extensive excavation of this and other French Missouri fur trading sites, Crosby has uncovered many of the artifacts that are displayed within the fort.

▲ *Fort Charrette is accurately restored and furnished. The porches are original and the brick chimney, though removed in the 1900s, was replicated from clues unearthed in excavation.*

Today, over six hundred school children visit the fort each year, and Crosby's parents operate an antique shop upstairs. They are open by appointment only. If you go, be prepared to take a fascinating trip back through time where you can touch the past to life and, in doing so, gain a better understanding and appreciation for the present.

▲ *The trading post was only open for business in the fall and winter when animal pelts were at their finest. When unfamiliar Indians were about, the chief trader closed his oak and hickory barred door and resumed his trading through a teller's window.*

▲ *The fort contains an extensive collection of seventeenth, eighteenth and early nineteenth century American woodworking tools. From felling and mortising axes, to crosscut saws and string line, these are the tools that built a nation.*

◄ *Antique crocks of all sizes fill a corner of the restored trading post. These, and thousands of other items in the old fort are for sale today.*

Seven Oaks

Although Crosby relishes the time he spends on his own pet projects, he makes his living finding, restoring and adapting log homes for other people. To embark on such a project is not a casual undertaking, and while homeowners often take an active part in their own house raisings, it is essential that they begin with a solid set of logs and well-thought-out drawings.

Old hewn buildings are getting very hard to find, and not every building will be salvageable. Just because a house has been covered with siding doesn't mean the logs are sound. House hunters should ask if they can take the boards off and dig around. Crosby cautions that plenty of people out there will take advantage of the inexperienced.

Once a building is located, the logs need to be labeled if you plan on putting them back together in the same fashion in which they were originally found. Whether doing a restoration or creating a new design, you'll need a solid foundation, a thorough knowledge of log construction and a firm commitment to energy efficiency. Early buildings could be drafty and cold, but with the proper application of insulation, vapor barriers and masonry chinking (for authenticity, Brown never uses synthetic chinking in his restorations), there is no excuse to build an energy inefficient home.

Like Crosby, most of his clients are motivated by a desire to connect with the past. When Chuck and Kathy Davis moved to the country from a suburb of St. Louis, they had never seen a log home. The couple had previously lived in a restored brick house, but it had been in a contemporary setting. In searching for a building to showcase their primitive antiques, they fell in love with the hand-worked wood of hewn logs.

Today, they contrast their log house to those in more contemporary subdivisions and note the tendency toward big homes, large rooms and useless space. They, on the other hand, appreciate their small, cozy rooms. The hand-hewn logs are personal and inviting, and they have only to look at them to sense and admire the presence of an earlier age.

◀ *Early hewn-log homes typically had wide chink lines. Because log movement causes air infiltration, this area and the corner notches are a home's Achilles heel. Still, Crosby shuns today's popular synthetic chinking products in favor of the real McCoy. Because old logs are well seasoned, cement chink may be used successfully when properly applied.*

▲ *Completely redesigned, this house was crafted from a barn built in 1840. This two-and-a-half story adaptive restoration mimics late Federal style and includes a full walk-in stone basement.*

▶ *This wraparound porch is an integral part of the home's design. For the Davis family it's like another room with a great view. They even enjoy it in winter when they bundle up to watch giant chunks of ice floating in the river below.*

▲ *The master bedroom contains one of four fireplaces served by double chimneys. Crosby used nineteenth century brick and built all the walnut mantles in the late Federal style.*

▶ The kitchen is housed in a small frame addition on the back of the house. Though not log, it incorporates hewn ceiling beams from the original barn. A turn-of-the-century, cast-iron Majestic stove is used more for heating than cooking, but it can always be counted on in a power outage.

New Homes Reclaimed From the Past by Charles McRaven

Charles McRaven (or "Mac" for short) has been in the business of restoration since childhood. He was eleven when his father put him and his brother to task on their first log cabin, and thirteen when they built a house of stone. As the author of books including *Building the Hewn Log House, Country Blacksmithing* and *Building with Stone,* he has deeply immersed himself in both the history and process of the prototypical hand-wrought home. Mac notes his experience is born of blistered hands, infinite patience and judgement sharpened in use. Over the years, he has restored many log buildings and Mac says there is no task — from forging nails to hewing logs and riving shakes — that he has not done.

McRaven, with his wife, Linda, who is very much a part of his business, jokes that they have earned the unenviable reputation of being able to salvage and restore anything! While Mac knows the limitations of his craft, his proven abilities have led people to call upon him when other contractors deem things hopeless.

A restoration, however, is never an uneventful experience, and Mac explains that it is not for everyone! Not only can the work be expensive, but it is time consuming, messy, and for the greenhorn, it can be exasperating. Still, for the individual who knows what runs true through Mac's veins, the log home experience will be a "delicious and varied affair."

▲ *This two-story home built by Charles McRaven for Ken and Ann Pankow combines two separate cabins. Ken bought the larger cabin dirt cheap for $500, but he wasn't allowed to rip the clapboard off to examine the logs. As it turned out, several of them were rotten and had to be replaced. That shot his costs way up, but there was some consolation since he also discovered a fine old six-board blanket chest inside that was worth nearly as much as the logs.*

◀ *A stone addition with heartpine post-and-beam work adjoins its hewn-log counterpart at the stairs in the McRaven home. Because stone is an extremely poor insulator, triple-wall construction with an insulated inner wall is used.*

Mac recommends that once you decide to undertake a project, your first step should be to contact someone who knows the ropes. You'll need logs and it helps to operate through an existing network. States like North Carolina, Ohio, Kentucky and West Virginia may be your best bet, but because logs from early homes are now harder to find, people are also turning to old tobacco barns, warehouses, and corn cribs for materials. Unless you plan on doing your own work wage-free, don't plan on any bargains. At this writing a restored log home in the East could be quite reasonable at $55-$65 dollars a square foot, but if you are committed to handcrafted authenticity in the finish work, the bill is more likely to be double that.

▶ *Charles McRaven's own house is a masterful example of the skills he has perfected over a lifetime. While still under construction, this two-story house combines a hewn-log restoration with the timeless addition of stone.*

Diamond Notched in Virginia

In 1865, the Civil War was coming to an end. On April 9 of that year, General Robert E. Lee and his confederate troops surrendered to Ulysses S. Grant in the little country settlement of Appomattox Court House, Virginia. Not far from that historic site, log-house hunter Lewis Ramsey found the unusual diamond-notched cabin that Richard and Lynn Rubenoff incorporated into their home. The cabin, probably older than either Lee or Grant, was believed to have been built in the late 1700s. Etched in a cornerstone on the home's chimney was the phrase "bilt in 1819," but experts know this was a second chimney, stacked after its predecessor had crumbled from decay.

With nearly fifteen layers of wallpaper inside and heartpine boards nailed to the exterior, the cabin's hewn, intricate diamond-notched logs endured both time and the elements. For the Rubenoffs, this venerable log cabin find became the home's "warm and cozy" centerpiece, around which more contemporary, open and airy rooms were arranged.

▼ *Intricate diamond-notched corners were an uncommon find. Though appealing, they are more labor intensive, and may have been more experimental than not.*

▲ *Lynn and Richard Rubenoff's home is a picturesque combination of log, frame and stone, but the small hewn addition in front, restored by Charles McRaven, is the focal point.*

▲ *A garden emerges in this little girl's bedroom where the logs stop and the walls begin. The original wide-plank heartpine floors are over two hundred years old.*

▲ The key to solid stone work is well-placed, tightly fitting rock. While true drystone is laid up without mortar, this fireplace is actually well-sealed to meet codes, and the mortar is tucked out of site. The fireplace was built by Hugh Larew.

▲ *This split-level home, built on a hillside, accommodated the ideal floor plan for two-family living. Both upstairs and downstairs open to the view and each floor includes a master bedroom suite and living room with its own fireplace. Here the upstairs bedroom opens to the back deck and to a hot tub that is just out of view.*

The Cabin at Wintergreen

Elaine and Michael Clayman and Bonnie and Harold Fagan had been long time friends when they decided to pool their resources and build a year round vacation home in the four-season resort at Wintergreen, Virginia. When they specified chestnut logs in their design, Mac had to do some searching. Chestnut, a once common eastern wood, was almost completely eliminated by blight in the 1930s. After two months, McRaven finally located the wood in an old double-pen barn. With more than enough material to build the split-level home designed by the owners, their architect Gilbert Jerome and the McRavens, the project got

▼ *Bonnie Fagan, herself an interior designer, wanted to convey a "sophisticated country charm" in the decor. Lighting was very necessary too. After spending too many vacations in dimly-lit cabins, both couples were determined to light this retreat as if it were their primary home!*

▶ *The stenciling in the dining room was designed by Bonnie and painted by another artist on the newly sanded heart pine floor. Next came a coat of polyurethane sealer and a layer of wax.*

▼ *The McRavens always leave their clients with a hand-crafted front door, complete with hinges and latches, forged by Mac in his blacksmithing shop. In this case the door was made from recycled wood known locally as "naily pine." The black spots that pepper the wood are the trailings of old nails removed when the boards were remilled. Naily pine is also used as trim throughout.*

underway. Bucking tradition, the design incorporates several large windows and French doors. Although less authentic, nothing has been sacrificed in terms of warmth. Today the two couples and their children continue to enjoy each other's company at this mountain hideaway when they can, while tourists rent it at other times of the year.

◀ *The Snyder cabin had been finished less than a year-and-a-half when they decided it was time to invest the money to relocate a bothersome telephone pole that was too close to the building. Although the pole had been there since 1939, the unsuspecting engineer figured the nicely weathered house had been there longer and moved the pole for free! For Mac, it was the ultimate compliment.*

Beaver Creek Farm

When Nan and Gerry Snyder bought their farm near Cismont, Virginia, they planned to restore the 1880s farm house on the property — until it flooded and they discovered how much it was going to cost. Their next move was in the direction of new log homes, but those seemed to lack character. That's when they stumbled into Charles McRaven and a whole culture of people doing the kind of work that fit so neatly into the little micro-cosmic world they had planned for themselves.

This typical "one-over-one" design is tiny and compact. One room downstairs is for living and the half-story upstairs is for sleeping. Rebuilt in 1989, the Snyders vacationed here every weekend for two years with only an outdoor privy and pump. "It was fine in winter," says Nan, "but the hot, sticky summers left us with an appreciation for running water." So, in 1990, they "modernized" with the frame addition of a proportionately teeny kitchen and bath. Although originally planned as a guest cottage, the Snyders have no plans to move.

▲ *The owners like old country and Nan has steered her furnishings in that direction. The homespun quilt on the bench against the wall was a housewarming gift from Linda McRaven.*

▶ *Although the screened porch wasn't original, it was too important to do without. Nan laughs that she's not a city person though she's lived in one the last thirty years. Out here, surrounded by their gardens, the birds and the cows, she's truly at home.*

The Adirondack Legacy

Today the six-million-acre Adirondack Park exists in the midst of one of the most populated areas of the United States. Developed in the 1800s as a recreational area for some of America's most affluent families, these woodlands are home to the elaborate and unique building form known as Adirondack Camp style. While it is the common folk who produce our most significant and enduring architectural forms, it's the wealthy that produce our most entertaining and triumphant. New York's Great Camps of the Adirondacks easily represent the latter.

Although an indigenous rustic style was already emerging in the secluded Adirondack region, it wasn't until William West Durant arrived on the scene in the 1870s that the significant elements of Great Camp style were defined. Durant, succeeding his father as president of the Adirondack railroad and developer par excellence, built a number of self-sufficient, multibuilding complexes characterized by the use of logs, bark, stone and highly decorative twig work. The resulting buildings and their furnishings were as much exquisite and handcrafted as they were raw and unrefined.

There was nothing unrefined about the clientele, however, and when families like the Carnegies, Vanderbilts, Morgans and Huntingtons retreated to their own woodland showplaces, dozens of servants were on hand to attend their every need. In an extended building system that more often resembled a small village, the weekend guest might find anything from a working farm, laundromat and chapel to a barbershop, casino and bowling alley.

Though these Camps, popularized in the Adirondacks, remained a largely local tradition, their legacy endured in the grand lodge architecture of the National Park Service. From there, of course, log homes continued their gradual upward spiral into the housing consciousness of twentieth century America. Today, we celebrate the Adirondack link and continue to emulate its imaginative architectural style in home and furniture design alike.

Sagamore and Pine Knot

▲ *Sagamore, completed by William West Durant between 1897-99, is generally regarded as his grandest Camp of all. Howard Kirschenbaum, in* The Story of Sagamore, *links its design to the romantic images of James Fenimore Cooper, the Tyrolean Alps and the log cabin.*

◄ *The front door of the three-story, chalet-style main lodge, shows the rustic fabric of bark-on construction. The building is primarily frame-built with log siding to maintain the log cabin illusion.*

▲ *This bay window at Camp Pine Knot, papered with silvery birch bark, is decorated with twig work symbolic of the games and recreation that took place inside.*

◄ *Sagamore is currently operated as a conference center and is one of the few Great Camps readily accessible to the public. This round-log building, though a meeting room today, was originally the playhouse and casino. Note the half-log shed roof above the upstairs window.*

▲ *A bird's-eye view of Sagamore reveals the extensive complex of buildings — many of which are linked together by covered walkways. Though preserved today in its entirety, there was a time when Sagamore was embroiled in a battle for its existence. Purchased by the state of New York in 1975, it would have been destroyed to maintain the "forever wild" condition of the park. However, in 1983, after years of struggle, the voters of New York State approved a land exchange that changed its fate.*

▲ Durant's cedar-sided cottage at Pine Knot was built by William West for his father Thomas. The extensive birch bark papering on the ceiling, fireplace and furniture are distinctly Adirondack and typify the detailing that was found both outside and in.

◄ *Camp Pine Knot was Durant's first experiment in Adirondack Camp design. Built over a period of fifteen years, Durant added more elaborate and rustic designs as he went. The decorative rails and gable detailing on this building are representative of the imaginative architecture of the region.*

Savannah

The Adirondack Great Camps passed their zenith in the 1930s. Still, they remain as guarded marvels of construction and architectural imagination. Steeped in the history of the gilded age, most are not readily accessible to the public. Nevertheless, the Great Camp style provides a powerful storybook prototype that is both meaningful and fun.

The Savannah hunting lodge in New York State plays on the Adirondack theme with infinite enthusiasm. Through its new-to-look-old construction and interior design, it recaptures both the rusticity and elegance of a Great Camp retreat.

For the owners of this massive fifteen thousand square-foot lodge, it was important that it accommodate large groups while maintaining a residential scale. For architects Holmes, King and Associates of Syracuse, New York, the task was challenging but not insurmountable. Utilizing large, sixteen-inch-diameter logs and oversizing many of the building components, they brought the whole mass into scale. Roof lines were lowered, overhangs extended and numerous dormers utilized to make the building appear considerably smaller than it is. Even the roof shingles are thicker and longer for added depth and texture. The result is a home that can either sup forty guests at an expandable dining room table and sleep them in cozy, oversized bunks upstairs or provide intimacy and calm for the owners and their five children.

The entire project, from working drawings to house warming, was completed in a record eight months time—a feat that could not have been accomplished without the camaraderie between the owners, architects, interior designer and hundreds of other craftspeople and laborers. Working with lights, and into the night, the crews completed their tasks on time and produced a building that is likely to endure far longer than its aged finish already suggests.

▲ *Savannah Lodge, built by Majestic Log Homes in Colorado, successfully weds Adirondack tradition with the log building lore of the Rocky Mountains. This idyllic retreat sits on its own privately stocked game preserve. Ribboned by water and dotted with small ponds and a lake, there are more than five thousand acres of surrounding woodland.*

◄ *Beaver-cut ends on oversized, unpeeled logs are powerful elements in this rustic design.*

◀ *In less than a year, interior designer Chester Sagenkahn of Syracuse, New York, collected a lifetime of antiques. What he couldn't find old, he had made new to look old. Combining motif art with the skills of handcrafters and artisans from California to Florida, Chester and his small staff created interiors that beg to be explored.*

▶ *With antique toilets, fixtures and sinks, and shower stalls of formed tin or hand-etched copper, no two bathrooms in the house are alike.*

▲ *A series of screened porches on the back of the house line up for views of the lake. This one, accessed from the master bedroom, has designs on the floor casually hand painted by some of the workers on the job.*

▶ *A comfortable sitting area in the master bedroom suite opens to the sleeping area two steps up. Attesting to the genius of both architects and builders, the separate sleeping chamber with its prominent stone wall was pieced in at the owners' request after house construction was nearly complete.*

Casa Snow—A Fresh Twist on Tradition

The Adirondack style lends itself to adaptation and reform in this contemporary remake. No shaggy, dark logs here! In striking contrast to the camps of old, this home designed and built by Alpine Log Homes in Victor, Montana, utilizes white washed logs to create a clean, fresh look. Still there is no mistaking the Adirondack link, and the house is filled with the characteristic textures of birch bark and twigs.

The bark work made famous by William West Durant in Great Camp Architecture was most likely inspired by the rough, bark-sided Adirondack lumber camps, which, in turn, were derived from the wigwams and longhouses of indigenous Algonquin and Iroquois Indians. If you want bark work furniture today, your best bet is still with the handcrafters living in the Adirondack region of New York State.

▶ *This contemporary remake of an Adirondack camp is located in upstate New York. Painted window trim, decorative railings and a screened porch are all reminiscent of Great Camp style, but sparkling, whitewashed logs add a delightfully fresh twist. Not wanting dark, bark-on logs or the yellowed look of pine, the owners were pleased to discover this option.*

▼ *Casa Snow's comfortable family room teases the imagination with its almost whimsical application of birch bark railings, furniture and fireplace mantle.*

▲ *A variety of barks, including birch, cherry and cedar, are utilized in furniture making. Using both the inside and outside of the bark and splitting it, a variety of colors and textures can be achieved. This beverage bar in Casa Snow was built by applying the bark to a wooden frame then finishing the edges with twig work.*

All "Casa Snow" photos: Alpine Log Homes.

2 ᵴ THE WEST

▲ *Historic Trail Town in Cody, Wyoming revives the old West with twenty-six buildings dating from 1879 to 1901, one hundred horse-drawn vehicles and an extensive collection of frontier memorabilia. Completely assembled and restored by Bob Edgar and his wife Terry, Trail Town is open to the public from mid-May to mid-September.*

There is something epic about the West—something vast and heroic that is at once both mythical and real. It is a place of contrast and extremes—of deserts and mountains and space. When the early pioneers abandoned their settlements in the East to claim the frontier, they ventured anew into no-man's-land. It was wild and hostile, yet free. There was tremendous hardship, yet hope, and for some, the spoils of the virgin earth would make them rich.

In the rush for land, glory and gold, the settlers came in droves, bringing with them only bare essentials for travel and a few cherished possessions. The familiar was traded for the practical or the possible, and round-log cabins were both. Lacking time and patience, frontiersmen and their families threw together crude cabins by the thousands. Later, when these same families had earned the means to build themselves a more permanent home, milled lumber had arrived on the scene. Technology marched on, and many of these early log shelters (unlike their eastern hewn-log counterparts) were quietly reclaimed by the earth.

Not forgotten, however, were the miners and their camps, the outlaws and their hideouts, the racy saloons and the one-room school houses. Cattle, cowboys and the Pony Express fortified western lore. Buffalo Bill Cody catapulted the audacious West into legend with the debut of his sensational traveling "Wild West" show in 1883. With improved railway transportation in the early 1900s and a more accessible media, the West charmed itself into the pocketbooks of increasingly prosperous eastern tourists. Western towns were no longer dangerous or isolated outposts, and the dude ranch took on an irresistible quality, thus presenting an entirely new vacation adventure.

Today, the West, though friendly, is not completely tame. Extensive tracts of land remain in public ownership and millions of acres of unroaded wilderness present us with a unique opportunity to preserve the last of our frontier. You can still get close to nature out West, or lose yourself in the vastness of a Wyoming landscape. The rodeo and cowboy culture are revered as never before, and western grit is deeply embedded in the spirit of the progress-weary soul.

In the 1970s, contemporary log homes regained their foothold. And, while eastern architecture was part of the historic myth that added fuel to this rebirth, it was the innovation of western craftspeople that built the industry into what it is today. It was western forests that yielded vast stands of well seasoned, dead, standing timber, and western wisdom that first built off-site with round (not hewn) logs. Synthetic chinking was developed in this region, and western architects were first to silence skeptics with contemporary designs. Log homes reclaimed their dignity in this charismatic land, and for many of today's home owners, nothing but the West will do.

WESTERN TRADITIONAL

While the earliest settlers first ventured west thinking they might find a better life, their countrymen who followed knew they would! Not only had gold been discovered, but there was a wealth of other natural resources just waiting there for the pickin'. Land, timber and precious metals baited fortune hunters, and towns grew up wherever the dust smelled of money. Some of these places prospered and grew; others prospered then went bust. Still others, because of their remoteness, just sort of existed. People homesteaded the valleys, and small town businesses dug in their heels. The railroads came and went, but the city never followed. Today, places like Sun Valley, Idaho, Jackson Hole, Wyoming, and Aspen, Colorado, pepper the map and rate among the most celebrated resort areas in the world.

Mostly old ranching and mining towns, these areas are rich in western tradition. If you explore their rugged mountain valleys, chances are an original ranch house remains, or the wind still reverberates through the empty shafts of spent mines. In many cases, residents have embraced this local history and incorporated it into their homes.

▲ *Old farmsteads like the Amundsons' are seen with less frequency on the national landscape, but where they remain, cherished memories are not lost.*

◄ *In the main house, original sawn logs, stacked without chinking, provided flat walls that defied a log cabin look. A new fireplace was flued into an existing chimney and Merle's farmer friend next door did the rock work. Mary found the Victorian gingerbread over the mantle at a local flea market.*

▼ *Country furnishings and period lighting fixtures reproduced in the East create a comfortable, down-home atmosphere. The screen door came from another early building owned by the Farnlun family.*

A Restored Dairy Farm

In 1883, Smith Farnlun and his family were among the earliest people to homestead in Idaho's Wood River Valley. The area, famous first for its ponderous ore wagons, is now also home to Sun Valley. Credited with the invention of the chair lift in 1936, Sun Valley is now a prestigious destination ski resort.

Farnlun had a sizable chunk of land, and he and his family ran a dairy farm until most of the pasture was sold off for housing developments in the 1970s. The barn, house and cabins remained in family hands until Merle and Mary Amundson bought them in 1989.

◀ *Past the milk house with its unusual corner notching, the barn can be seen. Still the hub of the farm, this traditional building takes on many roles—from workshop, dance hall and dining room to a stand-in chapel for family weddings.*

▼ *The walls in the 1883 ranch house were once papered with a more attractive covering. Layers of old newspaper and burlap were added later for additional insulation.*

The barn, an anchor on a vanishing landscape, had long been admired by the Amundsons. When they bought the property, their first thought was to make it their home. Then, not wanting to give up the barn, they turned their attention to the other buildings in the compound.

The original ranch house, though still standing, was converted for storage in 1936 when the Farnluns modernized. The family's next house was built of three-sided logs flattened on top, bottom and the inside. Even though round logs were no longer desirable, partially milled trees such as these were commonly put to use during this era—especially in towns where local sawmills were already producing timbers for the mines. The corners, however, were posted instead of notched, and siding covered the outside. The floor plan included three tiny bedrooms and a single bath.

Initially, Merle didn't intend on doing much to the place, but once he rolled up his sleeves, he didn't quit until the house had been completely remodeled. The siding was removed, the logs sandblasted and the house gutted. With a re-engineered roof, a new rock fireplace and a redesigned living space that fused three bedrooms into one, the ranch house was born anew.

▲ *The original ranch house built in 1883 was not log. There was neither electricity nor plumbing, and the outdoor privy used by the family is still there. The log milk house in the background was built in 1900.*

Two other outbuildings on the property were also restored and converted into guest cottages—one, a combination bunkhouse and woodshed and the other, a milk house built in 1900. Both were constructed with logs, but the milk house had been reinforced with concrete inside. A hole had been cut in its floor, and milk products were kept cold in an irrigation stream that still runs underneath the building today.

The barn, too, was cleaned and restored. With a century's accumulation of packed manure, it took five power washings to freshen things up. A concrete slab was poured and stairs built to the loft. The granary in back was converted into a workshop and Merle added a ramp to the loft so that he could winch up the antique buggies and sleighs that he restores as a hobby.

▲ *Hip roofs aren't common on log houses since they are tricky to build. Yet, because the first homes in the nearby community of Ketchum had a European flair, and the owners liked this roof's traditional design, Mark applied it here.*

Croney Cove

In south central Idaho, the Wood River runs hot and cold. Where waters are fed by snow they are very cold, but where they run warm, you can bathe in them and heat your home. At the turn of the century, geothermal activity around the Blue Kitten Mine made it a far more enjoyable place to be. Not only could a fellow get a bar of soap, a towel and a hot bath for a nickel, but when clean, he could mosey over to Madame Maud's for a bit of fun with the ladies. There was a hotel and gambling casino too.

The Madame and her girls must have been a busy bunch when the mines were in full swing. One of three local mines, the Blue Kitten Mine had a sixteen-hole privy! Madame Maud's

▲ *There is an old china sink in the kitchen with early Chicago faucets that the owners salvaged and rebuilt. The cabinetry is Mark's handiwork.*

▶ *The kitchen is reminiscent of a Bavarian farmhouse with its cooking fireplace and traditional furnishings. The radiant-heat floors acquire their color from a treatment with muriatic acid and linseed oil. The decorative wooden grids keep the large concrete slabs from cracking.*

establishment, known as Croney Cove, was developed by Maud Baugh after she purchased the site from the Warfield family in the 1890s. The first building on the property, a log "pool house," had been built by Mr. Warfield for his arthritic wife.

Today, Mark Hankinson and Lisa Vierling have rebuilt on the site utilizing as much of the original material as possible. Only a

crumbling chimney stood where the hotel had been, but the pool house, cat house and root cellar were all resurrected. The one-room pool house had to be dismantled and reconstructed with a new roof, floor and windows, but when it was finished, Mark and Lisa lived there for a year-and-a-half while they designed and built a new home on the property for themselves. Mark, having specialized in the construction and restoration of log buildings for more than half his life, did much of the work. Their main house, though rustic and built with logs, is somewhat of a departure from the simpler structures in Croney Cove. With a hip roof, it is more European in design, as were some of the earlier buildings in the nearby community of Ketchum. Lisa says it was a challenge to blend the two architectural styles, but by leaving the bark on saddlenotched logs and using chamfered-end cuts similar to those at Croney Cove, the two mountain-home traditions work well together.

Taking full advantage of local geothermal energy sources, the house derives all of its hot water straight from the ground. The radiant-heat floors likewise obtain their warmth from the hot springs. Mark and Lisa wanted to maintain a sense of the past and though the house is modern, it is not completely conventional. A dishwasher or disposal will not be found in the kitchen, and all the home's faucets and light fixtures are antique—some were even salvaged from Croney Cove's dump!

▲ *The authors' son enjoys a dip in the hot tub perched on the river bank. This old horse trough and a second, more elaborate sunken tub are just outside the pool house door. Although they don't have to, Mark and Lisa still prefer to bathe outside—even in winter.*

◄ *When Croney Cove's original log pool house was restored, there was no plumbing or electricity. Mark and Lisa lived there for a year-and-a-half making use of a wood cook stove, outhouse, and hot tub filled with spring water. The winters can be bitter cold and, for Lisa, the experience put her in touch with the able-bodied woman who lived there before her.*

▲ *The log walls inside the new Croney Cove house use quarter-round saplings instead of chink. The Rumsford fireplace, built with local granite, is named for the English count who designed it. Its large opening and angled back direct heat into the room instead of up the chimney.*

COWBOYS AND INDIANS

It seemed that every two-bit town in the American West had a story to tell—or a story that could be told if you stretched it just a bit. As our country aged, this western reality was both tempered and enhanced by the colorful exploits of nearly real people in very real places. Frederick Remington and Charlie Russell painted cowboy-and-Indian heroics. Esteemed villains like Billy the Kid and Jesse James were immortalized in the printed word, and the fabricated tales of Roy Rogers and Hopalong Cassidy put stars in the eyes of millions of would-be cowboys and girls. The media whipped the West into myth and made it larger than life. Adventure seekers came to hunt and fish and ride the range. The legendary "dude ranch" was packaged for the public, and people liked what they saw.

Evoked by tourist-inspired, great park lodges and the working ranch turned resort, a western style evolved that laid claim to the instruments and products of genuine cowboy and Indian culture. But it did so with a whole lot more comfort and ease. This style was as much or more a function of interior design as it was of exterior architecture, and colorful Navajo blankets and beadwork, cowhide and tanned leather, horns, iron accessories, Indian artifacts and, of course, rustic furniture were all important ingredients.

Today, as people reconnect with the log home experience, the old West is enthusiastically embraced. Historical and whimsical, the cowboy-and-Indian motif fosters the romance and casual elegance of our wildest dreams.

Molesworth High Style

There is perhaps no one man who contributed more to the development of western style interiors than Cody, Wyoming, furniture maker, Thomas C. Molesworth. Educated at the Art Institute of Chicago and influenced by both rustic Adirondack work and the Arts and Crafts movement, Molesworth created his own unique line of furniture that combined heavily burled wood with richly hued leathers, and vibrant Chimayo weavings.

As important as the furniture itself was the attention Molesworth lavished on an entire room. He designed complete interiors weaving a common thread into everything from fireplace screens and chandeliers, to magazine racks and ashtray stands. Gaining widespread recognition in the mid 1930s, Molesworth was commissioned as a furniture maker and interior designer by dozens of affluent families, grand lodges and prominent hotels.

The George Sumer Lodge, eventually purchased by the Bayoud family in Glenwood Springs, Colorado, displays the genius of the artist at work. Today this captivating collection of Molesworth furniture remains the largest of its kind in private hands.

▼ *Many of Molesworth's wooden pieces were routed out with stylized designs or cowboy-and-Indian motifs. While he created many of these images himself, he also incorporated the handiwork of his contemporaries. A number of local and regional woodworkers, ironworkers, and artists contributed to the Molesworth ambience.*

◀ *Dark brown paint, ragged, beaver-cut log ends and green window trim are all reminiscent of early western National Park Service buildings. The catch here is that the Bayoud's log home was first designed and built in Minnesota. Delivered by rail in the 1930s, this lodge takes exception to the notion that the expansion of the railroads put an end to log cabin living—then again, this isn't exactly a cabin!*

▲ *The Bayouds' great room is dressed from top to bottom in Molesworth high style. Sturdy, streamlined pieces are at once rustic and cosmopolitan attesting to a dualism in design that Molesworth so tactfully pulled off.*

◄ *Ponyskin curtains hang on wrought-iron, arrow-shaped rods. The colorful beadwork trim was hand fashioned by skilled Native American women working on-site in the home's kitchen.*

▲ *There was an element of surprise built into the Molesworth style, and he liked to have fun with a house. Each of the lodge's nine bedrooms are decorated around a different theme. Here, the Indian chief room (which shares a bathroom with the Indian princess room) includes routed images of the room's namesake in each major piece of furniture.*

◄ *An enclosed porch runs the length of the house, and visitors enter through the iron screen door that exhibits the sometimes elaborate— sometimes lyrical scenes that Molesworth commonly incorporated in his iron work. Patterned terrazzo floors and leather fringe furnishings, complete with brass tacks and Chimayo woven upholstery, hint at what's to come in the great room beyond.*

A Slice of Western America

Western style, like much that is American, is not cut and dried. One culture blends into the next, mingling form, fashion and tradition. For home owner Katherine Rosos, this house is actually many things. A strong cowboy and Indian motif spills over into Southwest design. As an artist and classical musician, Katherine spans this gap through her fascination with the music and rituals of Southwestern and Plains Indian cultures.

First and foremost to the home's design is the great room. Katherine wanted to create the feel of a lodge with a central area for performing, socializing and rough-housing. She believes that art objects should not be so precious that you can't live with them, and proves her point throughout the year by hosting some of the most popular children's parties in the valley.

◄ In the West, the nostalgia and appeal of park lodges like those created in Yellowstone and Glacier National Parks runs deep in the American psyche. Here again, we see the influence of those impressive early designs. For the owner, the lodge signifies a gathering place where people enjoy themselves. Intersecting gable roofs, dark-stained logs, green trim and a large impressive entry all prepare you for that experience inside.

▲ In the Rosos great room, Pendleton blankets and Navaho textiles splash color over pig-skin suede upholstered sofas and chairs. Contemporary Taos Pueblo drums serve as end tables, and a folk art totem pole and Indian-head dart board add a bit of whimsy. Iron tipi chandeliers were inspired by Molesworth and created by Mike Patrick in Cody, Wyoming.

◄ An Assiniboine woman's fully beaded dress yoke sets off a log wall in the living room. Thousands of tiny seed shells, and a fringe of cowrie shells on tube beads combine to create this stunning piece of handiwork. The Assiniboine people in Canada are related to the Blackfeet of the Northern plains.

▲ *Light seeps through the slats of Southwestern styled latilla doors.*

▲ *Just inside the entrance, an antique, cottonwood pueblo ladder leans against the wall. Accessorized with a vintage Pendleton blanket, tooled Navajo medicine man's pouch and an adorned leather headstall, this historical display suggests the cowboy-and-Indian cultures of both North and South.*

▲ *Kachina dolls were the symbols and teaching tools of the ancient Hopi religion. Carved originally from cottonwood root and colored with mineral paints, parents used these dolls to teach their children about the spirits and rituals that governed Hopi life. Katherine's collection seemed to warrant special treatment, and the master bedroom takes on a distinct Southwest flavor. Navaho rugs, and a 1920s painted Apache deer hide complete the scene.*

▲ *Owner Dale Launer is in the movie biz, and for him, there is definitely a theatrical sense about the fort. "Not only that," he says, "but it's a hoot! Adults will stand there and tell you it's a great place for kids, but you can tell by the grins on their faces that kids aren't the only ones they're talking about."*

The Fort

The imagined West was a wild and dangerous place. Fearsome Indians rode roughshod over helpless caravans of traveling migrants. With flaming arrows and piercing cries to battle, warrior braves swooped down from the mesas, only to be stopped short at the onerous doors of the cavalry stockade. Of course, Indians got the short end of the stick in white man's western lore, but that doesn't diminish the significance of the mighty fort. Sometimes, as the only stop on the outlaw trail, the forts were an important monument in western settlement. Many of these forts were built of logs, stood on end, and lined up into formidable walls that met with lookout towers or block houses at each corner.

There aren't a lot of forts around today, apart from restorations or Hollywood style recreations, but there is one in the Colorado Rockies. Straight from the pages of history—or better yet—a Louis L'Amour novel, this fort dishes up a powerful visual image along with a little fun.

▲ *These unpeeled logs are as rough as the cowboy characters of old. Steer hides and horns, the colors of Pendleton and an armadillo dish go with the territory. Look closely at the walls, and you'll even find an arrow or two leftover from last night's Indian raid.*

SOUTHWESTERN INFLUENCE

One of the most enduring forms of architectural expression found in the Western world has its roots in the southwestern part of the United States. This vast, fluid landscape has been inhabited by people longer than any other part of the country. More than two thousand years ago, Anasazi Indians lived here in the lap of Mother Earth, and it is in their ancestral past that contemporary Southwest architecture is rooted. Anasazi cliff dwellings gave way to sculpted adobe pueblos adapted and improved upon by the related cultures of the Pueblo, Navaho, Hopi and Zuni peoples. Spanish and American colonization added new elements to this architecture, and it continues to be characterized by its adobe walls, carved wooden doors, beamed ceilings, sculptured fireplaces, and view-conscious windows. Today, this building style (also referred to as Santa Fe design) is comfortable enough with its own heritage to be adaptable, and it is continuously expressed in new ways as its sphere of influence grows far beyond the confines of the Southwest.

Traditionally, logs played a relatively insignificant role in Southwest design. Because of their scarcity, they were used sparingly in the roof systems of early adobe dwellings. Small logs called "vigas" were laid across the tops of walls like rafters or ceiling joists. Smaller poles or branches called "latillas" were placed across the vigas, sometimes in diagonal patterns. Above this, earth or mud was layered to form the roof. Since adobe construction was worn down by rain and weather, the buildings needed constant maintenance. Many did not survive, but the precious vigas were always salvaged for use in new construction. In cases where the old poles were too long for their second

generation homes, they were allowed to extend through the walls. These projections came to symbolize Pueblo adobe design, and they persist in Southwestern architecture today.

As the railroads and sawmills made processed wood more available in the region, its use was reflected in vernacular style. Milled boards replaced tamped, earth floors. Window and door lintels were added, sometimes with ornate carvings, and posts with elaborately worked corbels were incorporated in the design of "portales" or porches. What began as fully earthen construction eventually progressed to a combination of wood and adobe. And, as log home living became more popular, logs presented an artful compliment to the organic forms and natural tones of Southwest design.

In this context, we present three homes designed in the spirit of the Southwest. Though hybrids by ancestral definition, each structure melds log into stucco with the richness and familiarity of the dramatic Southwest.

▲ *Early evening twilight adds its color to the glow from a sculpted beehive fireplace. Sandstone floors and built-in benches or "bancos" delineate intimate space in this enclosed patio designed by Darryl McMillen.*

Santa Fe Meets the Northwest

Since numerous large trees were unattainable to early Southwest builders, a full round-log home such as this one designed by Idaho architect Darryl McMillen would have been unlikely. There were probably some exceptions—particularly in areas near stream courses where trees grew in abundance. Even then, the logs were likely to be cottonwoods or some other ill-suited species that were best relegated for use in barns, outbuildings and corrals. Today, however, the western phenomenon of logs falls easily into step with other recognizable Santa Fe traits, and it would not be unusual to find this kindred offshoot in either mountains or desert.

▲ *The Spanish introduced the decorative carved corbels or "zapatas" on porch posts. Rounded courtyard walls are reminiscent of earlier adobe enclosures whose initial angular, earthen corners were softened by wind and rain.*

◀ *While early Southwest architecture dictated flat roofs, the influences of American colonization saw the advent of peaked roofs and gables. This variation provided far greater protection from weather and increased a building's longevity. Such a roof design was practical for this mountain home, but the architect retained traditional flat-roofed portales and adobe courtyards to lend more historical precedent in the overall design.*

▲ *Stark, flowing walls lighten interior spaces in true Southwestern form. Unpretentious furnishings are accented by familiar colors and textures.*

▶ *A complex array of log roof-beams makes for interesting geometric patterns. This roof structure was particularly difficult to build because the logs and connections are meant to be structural as well as visually pleasing. Author Art Thiede and handcrafter Norin Borke directed the log work.*

▶ *Pole slats in this popular style of door mimic the "latillas" in Santa Fe design.*

▼ *Anchored in a sea of native willows and tall grasses, the logs and taupe colored stucco of the McDorman house harmonize with the creeping hues of fall.*

Geometry in Log and Stucco

The geometric cubicles of adobe pueblos are crisscrossed with the lineal forms of logs to create an unusual house that is both comfortable and environmentally sensitive. Architects Jim Ruscitto and Thad Blanton worked in concert with owners Bill McDorman and Barbie Reed to combine logs, stucco, rock and glass into an extremely efficient passive solar design.

Two structural log walls intersect like a cross and divide the house into quadrants of stucco and glass. Log ends extend out into the surrounding yard to create a series of private courtyards.

The house with its earth-colored walls is built on pilings over a small stream, and lush groves of willows embrace the nonintrusive structure.

A wide-open floor plan, native granite floors, log posts and light-filled rooms speckled with greenery give the home a sense of the outdoors. Bill owns a high altitude seed company, and the house incorporates a solar area off the family room where vegetables grow year-round. The hot water tubing that heats the rock floors also warms the soil in a trough that extends to the outside.

◀ *The simple door, elongated windows and*
exchange of geometry and color.

This seat is creatively sculpted i
▶ *below. From different ways by*
a dozen different ways by

▶ *The home's*
combines
the c

▶ *Both the home and its furnishings reflect the McDormans' great*
appreciation for the creative labors of the handcrafter. This unusual
chair, named for Medusa—a mythological creature with snakes for
hair—was designed and built by Don King in Challis, Idaho.

...to the massive log post that supports the loft from ... look down into the living areas or eye the view framed ... the solar conscious wall of glass.

... interior is warm and light. As the owner of an art gallery, Barbie ... unique blend of contemporary and traditional furnishings that enhance ... comfortable Southwest ambience. A free-floating staircase makes an impressive ... entrance from the loft, and the linear presence of logs lends visual stability.

▶ A series of four huge log columns in the entry rise to meet the loft with its shapely, curvilinear walls. The post on the right protrudes into the upstairs space, and its massive top is carved into a seat. There are five-and-a-half tons of local rock in the radiant-heat floors. This rock and three inches of concrete below act as a heat sink, absorbing the sun's rays in winter and radiating warmth back into the house. In summer, the sun passes higher overhead, but what heat is absorbed quickly dissipates in the cool mass.

▲ The kitchen with its clean, white cabinetry and maple counters builds on the home's unifying, contemporary Southwest theme. A planter inset behind the sink is the source of fresh herbs and edible flowers year round. Protruding log ends, though trimmed in a calculated fashion, appear random and natural.

▶ The log portion of the house is built in the chinkless, Swedish coped method where the bottom of one log is carefully hand-scribed to fit the log below it. Traditionally, this building method is done with green logs that shrink together in a tighter fit as the wood dries. In this case, the logs were already dry to minimize movement in the walls. James Reed directed the log work, but Bill McDorman acted as his own contractor providing much of the labor himself.

Mountain Shadows

Dramatic rock cliffs rise in a theatrical display before
gradually descending again into sage covered foothills.
Their towering presence and form was not to be ignored by
this home that rests in their shadow. In another variation
on Southwestern design, architects Jim Ruscitto and Thad
Blanton wed bold, graphic, Pueblo inspired forms to the
western dictum of logs. In this case, strong, linear planes of
stucco alternate with log as the house steps up and back
into the mountains. Private outdoor spaces hide in folds of
parallel walls that stair-step from the house to the yard.

▼ *The front entry places you in a tightly controlled space that rivets attention down a narrow hall into completely open and airy living areas. The river-rock fireplace draws you into the room, but high ceilings and transparent walls connect you to the world outside. Cowhide pillows, a horse hair ottoman, lamps with perforated shades of pigskin and weathered copper, and a hand-etched and painted coffee table accent the interiors designed by Suzanne Manookian and the owner.*

◄ *This layered, monolithic facade presents an intriguing, yet very private face from the street side.*

◄ *The rear of the house takes on a more contemporary western form with log posts and expansive walls of glass that open up to a mountain of rock. The columns of log provide an external framework that is not carried to the inside. Standing in front of the hot tub, is the owner's "sun man"—a rusted, iron sculpture that recalls the Indian cultures of the Southwest.*

▲ *The interior was designed with one space flowing into the next. The strong, curving geometry of the staircase stands out in sharp contrast to the dark, stained wall of logs. A rich, Turkish Kilim upholstered couch and rug set the sitting area apart from the kitchen.*

▲ *Taking a hint from the powerful wall of rock, the master bedroom submits to the view. Bold, unadorned furnishings stay out of the way. The Great American Log Furniture Company built the bed.*

▶ *Mark Swazo Hinds is a Native American from the Tesuque Pueblo. As a friend of the owner, he asked to paint on her wall. His mural depicts images of Southwest culture in vibrant colors matched to the home. The artist, owners and some of their friends personalized the wall with their own colorful painted hand prints.*

THE NEW WEST

Architecture moves with the times and takes liberties with its design. Because the American West encompasses distinct regions and spans generations, there is nothing necessarily pure about western style. It is more the sense of history and place to which people are so irresistibly drawn. As such, many contemporary log homes designed in the frontier tradition take on a variety of characteristics that best serve their owners' nostalgic or romantic views. It is not uncommon for one home to roll Great Camps, Pueblos, dude ranches and their Hungarian grandmother's antiques up into a single package that still imparts a western ambience.

These are the homes of the new West, and today they represent the imaginings of people all over the country.

Mountain Artistry

Just as a house impacts the space it occupies, so may the space transform the house. In the historic silver and gold mining town of Telluride, Colorado, a home could not be perched amid the radical San Juan Mountains without some exchange taking place. Like an old mine that steps up and into the hill, this home takes its cue from the area's colorful local history. Red rock cliffs and fluid forest in turn lend their majesty for a grand presentation.

This house designed by Theodore Brown and built by Alpine Log Homes for writers John Naisbitt and Patricia Aburdene, combines traditional and historical materials with the unexpected—window bucks are formed concrete, and the

windows themselves vary from squares and triangles to octagons and rectangles. Yet, while embodying many less than traditional elements in its design, this is every bit a mountain home. With a second, postmodern town house in Washington, D.C., John writes that they really wanted something comfortable, earthy and high-touch to balance a world of high technology.

◀ Telluride, according to the owner, is warmer and drier than much of the West with an orientation toward Santa Fe. That led them to incorporate an adobelike, hand-waxed plaster into their design to soften the mass of logs and bring light to the interior spaces. Likewise, their art and furniture take on Southwest flavor and character. The log and plaster stairway near the home's entrance mimics the "viga" and stucco design of adobe pueblos.

◀ The home is built of materials selected for their ability to age, and the rusty brown-orange of the Cor-Ten steel roof blends nicely with the logs and cliffs beyond. For the owners and architect, the whole project was an experiment that led them to research and discovery. In the end, John Naisbitt writes that "Logs are difficult, but when you take the time to understand them, to meet their demands, they live and breathe in a way that drywall and paint never can."

All "Mountain Artistry" photos: Alpine Log Homes

◄ *In this innovative Colorado home, a tower with a 360 degree view, and a multifaceted, pop-out solar space are contemporary and sculptural in form. Poles that criss-cross at the gable peaks are a Norwegian influence, but Native American tipis also come to mind in this detail that accentuates roof shapes in light of the surrounding mountains.*

▼ *The unusual geometric patterns cut into windows like this one in the kitchen, create light patterns that remind the owners of being in the forest itself. Southern yellow pine cabinets, Mexican chairs and tiled floors attend the Southwestern theme.*

Reflections of Summer Camp

Childhood memories come vividly back to life when Betty Kolosta talks about the house she and her husband David own near Crested Butte, Colorado. Growing up on a ranch, and the happy recollections of summer camp are reflected in this special hideaway constructed by talented builder Steve Cappellucci.

The owners were not strangers to Colorado, and they knew they wanted a log house off the beaten path. "It is out in the boonies, and you have to snowmobile in during winter." It's more a summer "camp" though, and was designed with warm weather rains and sunset picnics in mind. Covered porches, a big sunny deck and well-placed windows are in concert with their surroundings, while an old-fashioned asphalt shingle roof matches the forest greens.

▶ *For Betty, this house is "Ponderosa goes to summer camp." Old fashioned and ranchy with great Texas-style sleeping porches in front and back, it was designed through the cooperative efforts of architect Michael Helland, builder Steve Cappellucci and the owners.*

▼ *Friends and family are welcomed by this impressive entry of timber, speckled logs and glass. Steve likes the contrast of one wood form against the other and uses timbers to frame all his window and door openings. Inside, he adds skip-peeled poles to the trim as well. Steve also designed the plank door shown here. To prevent warping, solid, hand-textured boards are fit in a frame with open mortise-and-tenon joints.*

◀ *When Cappallucci moved to Almont, Colorado, in 1971, his first job was peeling logs. He discovered it was more interesting to "skip-peel" them and has been doing it ever since. Steve likes to build with three-sided logs because he can do more with them. Using a simple "butt-and-run" technique, then squaring off the corners, he creates notches that, from a distance, resemble dovetail joinery.*

"Part of the fun was in the creative process itself," says Betty. "Everyone who worked there brought something new to the project, and you could watch the ideas come to life." For Steve, creativity is a gift, and this home, handcrafted from partially-peeled, three-sided logs, pays tribute to his marvelous command of quality, detail, and design.

▲ *"This is a people home," says the owner, with children, dogs and mud welcome. Above all, everything had to be durable and comfortable, but Betty also wanted to bring in color and texture. Betty jokes that people often lighten logs with white walls and counters, but to her, "that's like walking into a big baked potato!" She prefers bright, durable fabrics, Indian blankets and accessories. The old leather couch was in her father's office, and Betty wrote her first check sitting on it. Comfy, overstuffed chairs and ottomans are upholstered in a tapestry-like fabric that wears like iron.*

▲ *The kitchen required some extra thought. At mealtime the owners like to get everyone into the act, and they needed a kitchen scaled for many hands. Their solution was to make the counters extra deep and leave a generous space between the sink and thirteen-foot island. Because everyone who comes to visit has a cooler they want to empty into the fridge, the owners included the residential version of a Traulsen refrigerator. Betty's roomy pantry is off to the right and the only interior skip-peeled wall is visible at that point.*

▲ *The owners call this room their "tree house," and Betty's favorite colors—green and red—bring out the best in the logs. The spacious room, with its high ceilings, is balanced aesthetically with large pieces of furniture. The La Lune Collection twig bed reminded Betty of the Adirondack Camps, and it was "love at first sight."*

▲ *The upstairs contains the loft and master bedroom suite. Though the Kolostas didn't want a loft, their architect won out, and it has become a special room in the house. From this vantage point, you can get a feel for Steve's fabulous, modified hammerbeam truss work. Iron collar ties (visible from the living room) keep the beams from spreading and are decorative as well. Mottled log purlins draw your attention to the timber framed roof, and a skylight brings extra light into the space.*

▶ *Fabric behind glass cabinet doors and wallpaper accented with a bird's nest border, combine with textured wood in the guest bath. Betty and Steve designed the cabinetry, and David Treadway built it.*

A Lodge at Flowers Mill

This contemporary version of a log lodge balances lofty spaces with oversized logs and large stones in two massive river-rock fireplaces. Designed by Ruscitto/Latham/ Blanton and built by Highland Log Builders in Canada, the house is a friendly adaptation of Great Lodge architecture. In each phase of design, the architects incorporate elements to trick the eye and bring the scale down to a human level. Bulky materials in balance with each other perpetuate the illusion. Meanwhile, light pours into the interior from window walls on two sides, and an overhead log bridge between the entry and great room bisects the space preventing it from being overwhelming.

▶ *Set in a grove of aspen and surrounded by high desert sage, the Melin home is built at the site of the historic Flowers Mill—one of the earliest producers of mining timbers in Idaho's Wood River Valley. The large structure incorporates a simplistic, steep pitched roof line that isn't busy or overpowering. Upstairs, from the inside, dormers help suggest the charm and intimacy of attic spaces.*

▶ *Indoor/outdoor willow furniture purchased at a local craft fair sits pretty amid the textures and colors of fall.*

▶ *Although the ceiling in the central gathering room towers thirty-five feet, comfortable, oversized furniture makes the space genial and inviting. Owners John and Deanna Melin didn't want a room reserved only for company, and everything is designed to cozy into or curl up on. The wall-to-wall rag rug was custom woven for the room.*

▲ *The master bedroom is a great place to pad around in your pj's or stretch out by the fire with a cup of tea and a good book. Interior designer Jackye Lanham says they tried to make the room "cocoon like." A hand-wrought iron bed is dressed in cushiony wool felt with horn buttons. Comfy chairs in soft alpine colors sit opposite a cut-down table from a nineteenth century Dutch pub.*

▲ Steel plates and bolts are carefully concealed in well-fitted log connections beneath the front porch.

▶ Bar stools built by Robb Craig Hink of Hailey, Idaho, reflect a little cowboy humor.

3 ~ CONTEMPORARY LOG HOMES

As a raw product of nature, logs are massive and earthy. By their very form they suggest a distinction between a synthetic world and something more complete. This is part of their tradition and attraction. But the architect and builder who chooses logs is not necessarily confined to narrow preconceived eastern or western motifs—nor do logs on the outside always dictate the ambience within. While many homes still secure their appeal through traditional or rustic decor, others successfully defy familiar bounds in furnishing and design. In these cases, some may wonder why logs remain the medium of choice.

As a building block of life, the tree is among the healthiest of materials. In *The Natural House Book,* David Pearson writes that timber and logs breathe; they naturally assist ventilation and help to filter and purify the air. They are warm to the touch, absorb sound and do not disturb the natural, subtle, electrical and magnetic fields like most other building materials. Logs are energy efficient too. With their mass intact, a well-sealed log home will absorb and hold onto heat in the winter, while insulating a home from it in summer. If you've heard otherwise, chances are the culprit wasn't the wood, but the way the wood was put together.

Individual and beautiful, each log tells a story of the forest and of time. Whether imprinted with the lacework of bark beetles or hand-peeled to a satin finish, a log home imparts a quality and texture that cannot be duplicated with conventional building materials. At the same time, the wood is adaptable, and in its powerful presence, other materials can be incorporated in pleasing and unusual ways.

These are reasons enough to choose logs, but perhaps more pertinent is the deeper desire people have to live in a place that promotes mental and spiritual health. This is the gift of the tree, and for many people, while their homes may reflect a twentieth-century lifestyle, the logs in their walls provide a comfortable, emotional link to the earth and a simpler, more wholesome time.

Each contemporary home is a unique personal expression of which logs are an integral part. What you choose to say with this flexible building medium is left to your creative genius, but before you begin, carefully consider all your options.

If you'll be using an interior designer, it is wise to include them from the start. Not only can they help you locate specialized fabrics and furnishings, but their experience may prevent important oversights and encourage design ideas such as the incorporation of a sound system, adequate lighting, ample storage space or the inclusion of special nooks for oversized furnishings. They can also help you plan display areas for your art.

It's true that you can stick anything in a log wall without noticeably marring the wood, and contrary to popular belief, you can hang a straight picture with a little clever manipulation of long and short nails in back. Still, not everything shows best on log walls, and you should take this into account.

Consider too, the color of your logs and furnishings and how those elements effect the mood of a room. Light colors can make spaces feel bigger while bright colors lift spirits. Color and texture, along with the size and style of furniture can also be used creatively to emphasize, balance out or downplay the logs.

Keep your environment and climate in mind and the way you'll be using your home. If you have active children or entertain a lot, design for durability and wear. Plan living spaces that accommodate the sun, and don't overlook porches, decks and other outdoor areas.

Above all, allow yourself the freedom to accessorize. Often times, it is the little extras that personalize a house and set it apart as your own.

▲ *The designer and owners didn't want anything to be overdone so they used plantation shutters instead of draperies throughout. These clean, bright window treatments don't compete with the logs and are easy to maintain.*

All "State of the Art in Colorado" photos: Alpine Log Homes

State of the Art in Colorado

Logs speak their own language, and when you stand inside a log home, there are textures, colors and smells that stir the senses. Canadian residents Ronald and Annette Oelbaum met with these emotions when they visited a log house under construction in Vail, Colorado. Yet, while they relished the feel of the logs around them, rustic was not their style. They left wondering if they could build something of their own with a more contemporary flair. Not long after, they challenged the architects and builders at Alpine Log Homes to find out.

The result was this twentieth-century home that builds on a discriminating, monochromatic theme. With natural "sun-washed" colors throughout, the home exudes serene, sophisticated elegance.

▲ *The Oelbaums were looking for a ski base when they bought their first vacation home in Vail, Colorado. Years later, they outgrew their small townhouse and traded it in for this avant-garde retreat set amongst the trees. Their front door, designed by nationally famous artist Sydney Summers, presents a fitting introduction to this unconventional design.*

▼ *A hip roof with concentric circles of logs heightens the ceilings over the living room, and all the wood is stained with a carefully blended almond finish. While updated, the power and texture of the logs is not lost, and clean, comfortable furnishings cast this well-designed home.*

▼ *In the family room the mood is more casual. Mostly through accessories, the owners brought in elements of Colorado and the West. The pool table was custom painted to match the room, and the felt was done in a darker taupe. When designing this home, the Oelbaums knew from the beginning what they wanted in terms of an entertainment and audio center. As a result, they were able to incorporate a fabulous sound system while concealing the wires and mechanics in the logs—the moral: plan ahead.*

◄ *Interior designer Paula Johnson likes to maintain a consistent theme throughout the house while still creating a surprise diversion in each room. Placed around the handcrafted dining room table are chairs upholstered in a wonderful, though typically old and Victorian tapestry fabric. You may not expect to see them here, but the soft colors work well with the room and its art. The rugs in both dining and living rooms were hand-woven for the owners in Kashmir, India.*

▲ *The kitchen is the heartbeat of the Oelbaum residence, and it's one of the first rooms you see when you enter the house. The sleek custom cabinetry is painted with a water-based product that looks like enamel. This process originated in Europe and is applied in much the same way as paint is applied to a car. Rounded corners and granite countertops are both contemporary and complimentary to the logs. Lighting, another key component of the home, was accomplished with high-density surface mounts since recessed fixtures are more difficult to do in logs.*

Hammer Beams and Whitewashed Logs

Several years ago, plans were in the works for a small log summer cabin on thirty-five acres of land near Steamboat Springs, Colorado. However, time, a second marriage, and a new affinity for winter changed all that. Today, this full family vacation house is enjoyed year-round, and though it's roomy, there are lots of friendly niches.

The house is planned around a two-story gathering space. A double stairway leads to an interior balcony that extends to three sides. All the rooms, both upstairs and down, open to the central living area and no one is out of earshot. Upstairs, a large master suite lies on one side and two children's bedrooms are on the other. In between, double French doors open to an outdoor porch and panoramic views of the Continental Divide.

▲ *On first glance you might see a ranch house or even a lodge, but the overall design really grew out of the home's interior floor plan. The logs are a powerful element in design so a simple gable roof built to withstand heavy snow loads works well. Inside and out, the logs are hand rubbed with acrylic latex stains for a silvery, weathered look. Brightly trimmed windows and French doors are expressive and lively.*

All "Hammer Beams and Whitewashed Logs" photos: Alpine Log Homes.

▼ Pesky and Lady wait for their owners under the porte-cochere in back. The cross gables of this log portico incorporate miniature versions of the same timber frame trusses inside.

▲ Overhead in the living room, modified hammer beam trusses are both structural and visually appealing. Built of fir, they do not have the pickled finish of the pine interiors. While the owners were specifically trying to avoid the yellow look of aging logs on their walls, these handcrafted trusses nonconform with eye-catching appeal.

▼ *A large bright window opens up the master bath and creates a center point for symmetry in design. Logs in the upper walls and roof do not pull away from the clean, contemporary elements of this modern space.*

▲ *According to the architect (who also acted as the interior designer), this is not a contemporary house as such. The owners are from Chicago, and the husband is a modernist. Yet, while they didn't want to lose that sense of log and history, neither were they slavishly tied to the past. The interiors combine the family's Italian sofas with iron, glass and granite-top tables. The furniture, while eclectic, is made of natural materials that blend with the wood.*

Country Victorian Remake

When Susan and Michael Niven purchased their log and stucco home in Idaho, they had one word to describe it: "Ugly!" Big, plain and boxy, this was not the home of their dreams, but it was a start. Looking past the facade, Susan saw high ceilings and wonderful southern light. The house wasn't large, but the rooms were all there and the "bones were good." While captivated by the logs, the fact that it was part stucco made it all the better.

Susan, an interior designer with a home base in Los Angeles, set to work with Ketchum architect Steve Pruitt, and local builder Steve Rath. Together they revived every elevation, extending the front of the house and adding bay windows to take advantage of the warm, bright light. The home took a departure from the traditional with a country/Victorian feel.

The whole project was a challenge and Susan points out that major log remodels are tricky business, especially in terms of electrical and plumbing work. "You don't just cut through a log wall like you would conventional sheetrock." But given imagination, time, and an adequate budget, a makeover can be an exciting and gratifying experience.

▼ *A covered patio area and spacious decks maximize outdoor living in this newly redesigned home. A river-rock privacy wall doubles as a planter that fringes summertime diners with a fragrant ribbon of color.*

▼ *A large, sunny, divided-light bay window provides a cozy nook for informal dining. Combining the sitting area at right, the whole kitchen/breakfast area becomes the entertainment center of the house. "In California," Susan says "they were painting the whole town peach and aqua so it was a relief to use primary colors to bring out the richness in the logs." Red was the theme color with blue and green accents. Simple swags replaced full curtains, enlarging the windows and allowing more light in.*

▲ *Susan points out that "so often in design, a problem can be turned into an opportunity." This foyer is a perfect example. As you walked through the front door of the old house, you passed through three separate, small, dark spaces. That all changed when spacious, arched openings were cut through the logs. A pie-crust mirror and carved bear now decorate another wall that was plastered over for contrast.*

▲ *The kitchen, as one of the larger, well-lit rooms, was the core of this house. Originally flat and drab, it had honey-colored cabinets against like-colored logs. Susan transformed the room with the addition of molding around all the doors and windows—a feature that extends throughout the house. The cabinets, also faced with molding, were painted white and chopping blocks were added to the counters. The garden room to the right is new and serves as a formal dining area.*

▲ *In the original house, the master bedroom was "a very small, tall room." A new window seat conquered the boxy feel and created a pleasant sitting area. To bring the sixteen-foot ceilings down to scale, the walls were essentially divided into thirds. Wainscoting was applied on the bottom, a small-print Ralph Lauren paper is carried up to chair molding in the middle, and the top section was painted a khaki color.*

Winfall

Typically, round log architecture has been a western phenomenon while hand-hewn homes with dovetail corners were more commonly found in the East. Chalk it up to tradition and the availability of the appropriate logs, but don't cast it in stone. Today, a growing respect for the art of dovetail joinery and a regard for flat walls has coaxed this historic building form West while adapting it along the way.

Feeling strongly that round logs were too busy and intrusive for a log interior, yet wanting to retain a handcrafted appeal, Win and Joanne Lauder opted for a hewn-log home. The house is built with massive, dead standing white pine—sawn first, then hand adzed on front and back. Jokingly named "Winfall" for the owner and the inheritance that helped build it, the home is located next to the library in downtown Ketchum, Idaho. Convinced that dovetail homes are a little more formal and architecturally simple, the Lauders had no qualms building Winfall in the midst of this bustling, commercial environment.

▶ *To maintain privacy, Win began this project believing that he would design a fort—four walls around an interior courtyard. But when the concept didn't work out on the elevated downtown site, he and Stan Acker patterned a home that, while retaining a courtyard in back, took advantage of the sun and views. Spacious bays pop out on both sides of the entry and a second set of windows down below send light to the basement.*

All "Winfall" photos: Norman McGrath

◀ *To help counter the mass of stacked wood, native Oakley stone was used liberally around the foundation and in the entry. A commercial grade steel roof with heavy battens was chosen over wood shakes for its durability and weighty appearance. Exterior beams are stained with Cabot bleaching oil that will act as a preservative while turning the logs a weathered, silver grey.*

▲ *The owners were delighted to find that logs were not the least bit restrictive in terms of decor. Interior designer Frank Penino wanted the logs to tell the story and chose muted colors that would not compete with the walls. Penino also designed the coffered ceiling with wire brushed cedar panels recessed beneath a sea-green, antiquated copper frame.*

▶ *Much of the home's character is derived from the handiwork of specialized local artisans. Jack Burgess built one-of-a-kind bench beds in the guest room out of white bark pine harvested on nearby Galena Summit. Sanded to a six-hundred-grit finish, they are as smooth as satin. Jack also fit the portal with a twisted branch and fashioned holders for the curtain rods.*

◀ *The kitchen is central to the home's open, flowing design. Decorative log work forms a lattice over a work area that sits like an island between the living, dining and family rooms.*

Storybook Charm

To build a large house would have compromised the intimate nature of this home and, for the owners, destroyed the magic of the logs. Unfortunately, that created quite a dilemma because this eleven hundred-square-foot cottage was never intended to be the "dream house" that it has become. The owners were drawing up plans for a rambling forty-five hundred-square-foot main house while indulging in fantasy and building what was to be simply a log guest house. As construction progressed,

however, the family nearly lost sight of the primary residence, and this little two-bedroom, one-bath cabin has since taken its place. With two small children, they will eventually need an extra bedroom, but this comfortable family retreat has really made them re-think their needs in terms of space.

The house sits on an island in the Pacific Northwest, and during construction, the family was delighted to discover that their home was built, nearly corner for corner, on the site where another log cabin had once stood. Old square nails, antique bottles and numerous other artifacts were unearthed that played into the same fanciful sense of mystery that had led the owners to try logs in the first place and "get them out of their system." Down the road, a midden, with the castoff accumulations of life in an Indian village, further enhanced the fascination of the place. Because of its historic significance, care was taken to preserve the area and construction of a road had to be delayed. As a result, the house was built with materials delivered to the beach by barge, and the log shell was up before you could visit the site by car.

◀ *This homespun, seaside cottage takes on an elfish quality through its tall, compact design. While small by some standards for an active family of four, the intimate spaces in this eleven hundred-square-foot cabin reward the owners and their children with high quality family time.*

▶ *A cathedral ceiling and white-stained logs brighten the tiny living room and give it a more spacious feel. Yet, because the room is so small and the ceiling so high, stringer logs were erected overhead to help scale the space without closing in the room. As the owners committed themselves to this home, they opted for luxuries that weren't planned initially—such as radiant-heat floors. Unlike forced air systems, they prefer the warmth radiating from below and enjoy the fact that it doesn't dry their skin.*

All "Storybook Charm" photos: Alpine Log Homes

◀ *Entertaining is a joy for the owners, and the kitchen is the biggest room in the house. Bleached wood cabinets, white Corian countertops and decorative handmade tiles are fresh and light. Large French doors here and around the house are open all summer long, and the rooms extend out onto the decks. A stone wall compliments the logs and adds an element of storybook charm.*

◀ *Large custom-made windows are important design elements from both a visual and spacial perspective. Here, the bathroom window fills the room and provides the best view in the house.*

Maple Island Lake Front

Until Carol and Edward Miller walked through the open, light-filled offices of Maple Island Log Homes, they had been content with their pre-fab log vacation cabin on Torch Lake in Michigan. Previously, adjectives like dark and heavy had always come to mind when they considered full round logs. That was before Carol's brother introduced them to Richard Tuxbury, a co-owner of Maple Island. He showed the Millers through his own custom home/office and let them compare richly textured, hand-peeled, scribed and notched logs to the milled and pre-cut logwork that they had known before. That was all it took, and the Millers are now rediscovering log home living in this retreat designed and built for them by the Michigan based company.

◀ *Emulating the model home that first inspired them, the living room is spacious and open. A bridge overhead connects upstairs bedrooms to a family room and play area. The house was designed with guests in mind, and the mood is casual and comfortable with easy-care fabrics and furnishings. Because the wood absorbs light and imparts its own color, Carol and her interior designer used bold patterns with visible texture. Rich, durable oriental rugs combine with rattan Ficks-Reed furniture that can be easily recovered should they want to redecorate later. A soapstone wood stove adds its warmth to sunlight that pours in through skylights and the window wall facing the lake.*

▲ *The Millers wanted traditional styling without traditional shortcomings such as undersized windows and cave-like rooms. Here, Maple Island incorporates classic line and roof overhangs in a design that includes a screened porch left of the entry, log railings, ample windows and additional skylights.*

▲ *Stairs step down the hill to the lakeshore. The two-story bay, a prominent feature on the back of the house, is covered with cedar-wood siding that blends into the logs. Latticework hides empty, under-deck space.*

A two-story bay is a functional and architecturally interesting aspect of this home's design. Built with conventional materials, the bay is visually tied to the home by the presence of log purlins. Extra space and a three-dimensional view make this niche a pleasant place to play games or relax. The room's extra-thick pine floors also serve as the ceiling from below, and if you look closely, you'll find a miniature version of the Miller's house in the lower left-hand corner. It was built as a bird feeder and gifted to the owners by Maple Island, but the owners value it too much to hang outside.

What Began as a Barn...

Logs, timber framed trusses, glass and sculpted plaster combine for a grand presentation in this Rocky Mountain home. Set on an original farmstead, the plans for this structure started out as a barn. The owners had always wanted to build something with logs, but stables— not a home—seemed to be the logical first step. It would have been magnificent too, had the price tag been more manageable. The cost was shocking, and the owners may have abandoned the entire project had their architect not suggested they rethink the design and live in it. That signaled the beginning of a wonderful, flowing process with the family and Conger/Fuller architects working in concert to coordinate the

ideas that sprang forth out of their rekindled excitement. The barn was stretched and turned, horse stalls were converted to bedrooms, and a cathedral-like great room took over one end of the house with tremendous arched windows that placed western scenery in majestic frames. The outside logs were stained a darker brown, and colorful green trim highlights the windows and roof line.

Once the log package arrived from Custom Log Homes in Montana, Jack Wilkie Builders took over and finished the house a year later. With everything on such a grand scale, the house presented special challenges. Even though the wood was dry, a small amount of shrinkage multiplied by so many courses of logs led to settling that could have cracked plaster and pinched doors and windows. Anticipating this in advance, every two consecutive logs were drilled and pinned with steel. Further steps were taken to prevent differential settling between the walls and vertical columns. Steel bearing plates were installed internally at the corners, and posts were set on huge adjustable plates that can be lowered when necessary.

◄ *Paired posts, scalloped corbels and raftertails, and exemplary wood joinery and pegging are all reminiscent of Greene and Greene architecture.*

◄ *A circular drive takes you under an open, four-gabled porte-cochere to the front entry. Scissor-beam trusses and scalloped raftertails reoccur throughout the home and provide contrast to rougher hewn logs. Off to the side, water trickles down a fountain built into a grassy knoll.*

▲ *This would-be-barn sits on a lush meadow overlooking a small pond. Though downplayed in evening shadows, the towering, round-top window in the gable end inspires awe—both in terms of its design and execution. The triangular skylight in the peak of the roof sends sunlight streaming into the rotunda at the home's core.*

◀ *Soaring space rises thirty feet to scissor-beam trusses and white plastered ceilings in this huge gathering room. For this family of nine, it was important to create a place where everyone could come together and feel at home. There was no particular theme except to keep things light and airy. With seven kids, twelve dogs and a cat, the wife laughs that endless creatures demanded a comfortable, lived-in feel. Interior designer Philae Dominick obliged with an eclectic array of "user-friendly" furnishings conducive to relaxing or entertaining. The room's central feature, a huge round-top window, is twenty-six feet high with three-foot window jambs that provide enough shear to stiffen the gable end. Motorized clerestory windows designed for light and ventilation are controlled from below.*

▲ *Despite the vastness of the great room, there are lots of comfortable corners where overstuffed sofas and chairs encourage you to settle in and put your feet up.*

▶ *Entering the home from the porte-cochere, you walk down a long corridor where horse stalls might have been. Art now decorates the walls, and seven doors lead into children's bedrooms along the way. The hall empties into a rotunda with a sweeping staircase set against one wall and a Japanese-like gate supporting the balcony overhead. You feel almost as if you are standing in a Shinto portal, but that was not intentional. Architect Michael Fuller says "that when you start out with the same materials and wood to wood connections, you arrive at a similar place without necessarily emulating another cultural style." At the gateway you look straight through the great room out to the mountains beyond.*

▶ *Off in one corner of the great room, the kitchen is set apart—sculpted out of soft flowing forms of adobe-like plaster. Not wanting an overabundance of log on the inside, the owners use this bright, pliable material throughout the house, but it is especially striking here. Handmade tile from Taos, cherry-wood cabinets and a polished granite slab on the kitchen island recall a sophisticated version of Southwestern architecture.*

▲ *Eccentric log trunks were handpicked in the forest by the owners and made into a bed for the master bedroom by building foreman, Donald Cramer. On the job, the crew fondly referred to Don as "old yeller" for his booming voice, but the contractor marvels at his creativity and ability to invent tools for tricky one-of-a-kind jobs.*

▶ *A small library behind the kitchen provides a cozy nook to read in or listen to music. Stucco walls are again used creatively to wrap up a built-in sofa, book shelves and Southwestern style fireplace.*

"Sandwiched" for Warmth

Eight acres of open meadowland with mountain views and running water provided all the necessary elements for this home near Jackson Hole, Wyoming. Featuring a pond and taking full advantage of high mountain sun, this log house maximizes energy efficiency. Owners George Payson and Gilman Alkire helped conceptualize their home designed and built by Logcrafters. This Wyoming-based company specializes in a form of super-insulated, "sandwich wall" construction that offers the benefits of both log and frame-built homes. The system uses milled logs on the exterior, two-by-six-inch stud walls with fiberglass insulation in between and a thinner cut interior log wall. The finished product is an extremely energy efficient home

with a traditional look on the outside. However, inside you can conveniently pick and choose where your log walls will go while playing them against other smooth or textured surfaces such as adobe, wallpaper or panelling.

◀ *Three-sided "D" shaped logs with butt-and-pass corners form the home's outer skin in this triple-wall approach to log house construction. The owners decided to grey their logs, and picked the trim color for its contrasting appeal.*

▼ *The simple, uncluttered kitchen and dining room take on the Southwest with lightly tinted pink walls, window lintels and an antler chandelier. The dining room table, however, is one of George's cherished antiques and has been in the family since his ancestors first sailed to America on the Mayflower.*

◀ *The house is basically a series of three cubes—the first containing the owners' bedrooms and baths, the second featuring a family room and guest bedroom, and the third and central cube with living, dining and kitchen areas. Off the living room, a solarium with four feet of river rock buried beneath its floor, incorporates a heat transfer system to circulate warm air through the house. As long as the sun shines, the home's radiant-heat floors are practically unnecessary—even on the coldest days. A grey metal roof set off by vibrant red trim was chosen over shakes for its sleek, modern appearance and ability to shed snow in this mountain environment.*

▲ *Adobe walls predominating inside are set off by hand-peeled log trusses and trim work. The furnishings are an eclectic mixture of modern pieces and good antiques—including some that have been in the Payson family for over 250 years. Black wool sofas face a large rock fireplace with doors that open to both the living room and dining room on the opposite side.*

▼ *In one of the bedroom suites, French doors open to south-facing decks overlooking the pond. The art on the wall was a by-product of house construction. When workers finished painting one afternoon, they saw the imprints of steel plates on composite board, but when the owners discovered the scraps destined for the dumpster, they salvaged it as modern art! The boots to the right of the bed belonged to George's uncle, Spencer Tracy, and the desk on the left is another early American antique.*

Designed For a View

Dennis and Leslie Frieder always wanted a lot with a panoramic view. When that dream became reality, they designed a contemporary home with a large circular window wall to frame the vistas around them. Built by Peter Dembergh and Alpine Log Homes, the effect is accomplished by the intermingling of two distinct building styles. Post-and-beam construction permitted the curving wall with large expanses of glass, while more traditional notched, horizontal log construction is used in back.

▶ *Radial rafters emanate from the river-rock fireplace in a dramatic display overhead. From the carpet and furnishings to the logs themselves, the Frieders chose light colors to create a "clean, contemporary Palm Springs feel." For the chimney, local mason Bill Baybutt travelled several hundred miles to locate a diverse selection of unusual rocks then laid them on end to accentuate their shape and markings.*

▲ It's been said before, but it's true: no matter how nice the living room is, everyone ends up in the kitchen. With that in mind, this area of the house is open and spacious so that once people settle in, they can pitch in with the chores! Rock-facing on the island is both durable and attractive. The slot machine on the left is a souvenir from Reno, Nevada.

▶ Not wanting a lot of harsh corners or points in their home, the Frieder's were attracted by the roundness of logs. As the major element in the home's design, the semi-circular wall of glass in front worked beautifully with the wood and the owners' overall concept.

4 CRAFTSMAN DESIGN

As with many creative endeavors, it is the finish work and attention to detail that sets one artist's handiwork apart from another. Log building is no exception, and the following chapter contains a group of houses that we loosely define as being of craftsman design. This term is not to be confused with the Craftsmen style of architecture that became popular in America during the early 1900s. Also known as the Arts and Crafts movement, that school of design embraced some of America's best-known architects including Frank Lloyd Wright, Bernard Maybeck, Gustave Stickley, and the Greene Brothers. Characterized by attention to detail, extensive use of handcrafted wood, intricate joinery and so on, the Arts and Crafts movement incorporated many of the features that we attribute to the homes featured here; however, it also spoke to a particular school of residential design that we do not. In this context, we use the term craftsman more in the objective role of construction than in the subjective realm of design.

Next one might ask, aren't all log houses by their very nature handcrafted examples of the wood butcher's art? And, if so, what distinguishes the homes in this chapter from others that are finely crafted? For us, many craftsman-designed homes seem to have a sculptural feel to them. Artisans have left their individual marks in some extraordinary ways, sometimes through intricate carvings on doors, posts, rafters or purlins. In other cases, the tree trunks themselves are exploited for their inherent artistic qualities with branches, cat's-eyes and burls highlighted for visual excitement. Stained glass, superbly crafted doors, furniture, fireplace surrounds, interior spaces, exterior design and more all combine to fashion this elusive, unrestrained form.

The tree is nature's perfect building block. Infinite in form, size, texture and color, the tree, or log as you will, can be used whole or milled and shaped into a variety of designs. Like a well worn pair of blue jeans or cowboy boots, the wood mellows with age and, depending on its finish and species, takes on a rich and varied patina. This quality, and the general care given to the logs themselves, is another characteristic of the craftsman-styled home.

During harvest and building, the logs are subjected to considerable abuse. Skidders, loaders, cranes and other mechanical devices all leave their marks on the surface of the wood. Sometimes, this is superficial and can be worked out by draw knives or sanding. Many times, however, the wounds are so deep they cannot be removed and remain as permanent scars. The commitment to retain a natural beauty starts in the woods and follows through to the last coat of finish. To say this is a significant task is an understatement given the volume of wood in a typical log home. For the dedicated craftsman, however, the results are well worth the effort.

Another significant factor in the craftsman-built home is the high degree of involvement among owners and builders. In fact, many times the owners are the builders. Rarely are these homes rushed to completion, and creative license is free to pursue its own circuitous path. It's virtually impossible to delineate every detail of finish in the initial design phases of a building, and nowhere is this more apparent than in a log home. Creativity, flexibility, experimentation, patience and true commitment to excellence all figure into the craftsman equation.

▶ *A life-size eagle alights atop her nest of hungry young in this spectacular stairway carving in the Neary home. Local artist Paul Stark carved the eagle from a solid lodgepole pine log. Knowing from experience where the stained "blue-and-buggy" wood would fall, he expertly worked it into the bird's wing tips, head and beak. The nest was carved from cedar to provide contrast, and a high-gloss finish on the wood adds to the sculptural effect.*

▲ *With the excavation of a pond and extensive landscaping, the Nearys transformed their ten-acre desert lot into a virtual oasis. The house overlooks the water and a pasture beyond where five pairs of shaggy, Scottish Highlander cows graze contentedly.*

▶ *This enchanting elevation maintains a deceptively low profile with its steep-pitched roof and multiple gables. Applying new technologies, the Nearys used a recently developed roofing material known as Perma-Tec. This concrete and fiber composition roof is less expensive than slate, stronger than tile, and equally fireproof.*

Return to the Nest

The Pacific Northwest is a land of remarkable beauty and extreme contrasts. Nowhere is this more evident than on the eastern slope of the Cascade Mountains. Towering over the high desert community of Bend, Oregon, are the inspiring peaks of the Three Sisters—a beautiful background vista for this award-winning home. As the first log house to win the prestigious "Best in America Living Award," this house incorporates a number of distinctive and finely-crafted features.

The Nearys—Mike, a self-taught builder and co-owner of the Oregon Log Home Company with his wife Laura—created and built this special home as their own. "We had a lot of terrific design ideas," says Mike, "but couldn't always convey them to our customers. That's when we realized we could build something for ourselves and show them!"

▶ *In the home's exterior, river rock is tastefully incorporated into the half-moon bay of the dining room and around the patio. The deck above is accessed off the study and has become a favorite summertime sleeping porch. Because harsh sun on the west and south sides of the building tends to break down the finish on the wood, logs were treated with four coats of Sashco Resin Lock, including two coats of pigmented, cedar-toned base.*

◄ With the logs already in place, Paul did this second eagle carving with a chain saw and chisel lying on his back atop scaffolding. Paul stylized wings across one twenty-foot beam and worked the body, tail and head into another. In this and other Neary-built homes, full log gables and dormers are rarely incorporated since even dry logs will shrink and loosen things up. Instead, they use log siding on the exterior and wain board within. In other areas of the home, they allow for three inches of settling.

▼ The use of naturally flared tree-base posts distinguishes this door frame.

▲ *Opposite the solarium in the same open space, living room furniture is oriented around the rock fireplace with its root-based mantle. Beyond that, a large arched passageway directs your attention to one of the home's most outstanding features—a spiral staircase. While difficult to build with conventional materials, logs present an even greater challenge. That, however, is only part of the appeal.*

▲ *The east side of the Cascade Range is blessed with many sunny days, a fact not ignored by the Nearys. Here, the solarium opens to the patio making this room popular in both summer and winter. Inside, all the logs were sandblasted, then three coats of lacquer were applied with hand-sandings in between.*

◀ *Root-base posts are used throughout the home—an inventive detail that makes these members look as if they are growing straight from the ground. Simple stone planters are tasteful extensions of the patio walls.*

Cat's-Eyes and Knobbies

There are many ways in which builders and designers seek to impart a signature to their work. And while no two logs are exactly alike, builder James Morton of Roberts, Montana, carries this a step further with the incorporation of natural and unique log forms that have become his trademark, and his company's namesake, "A Very Unique Log Home."

Building what James refers to as "crooked houses" has many challenges—not the least of which is finding the logs themselves. Morton searched for six years before discovering his secret "enchanted forest" on a remote, fog enshrouded mountain top.

With an ample supply of wood, Morton's company designs and constructs homes with as many or few character logs as his clients desire. He also goes to extremes to build tight, energy-efficient houses that are virtually fly proof! His secret is foam, and he wouldn't build without it. Dead standing pine is used in both chinked and Swedish coped homes, and logs are often reshaped to create supertight notches. Liquid foam is then injected at every conceivable point of the building, including along the ridge line and purlins. Chinking is applied, and cracks are caulked and re-caulked until the job is absolutely perfect.

◀ *In this home built for Doug and Debbie Speer, there were eight flies last year—though Morton's techniques have since improved! The Speers loved the knobbed logs, and James used them liberally inside and out. Burled logs in the entry and a forked log inserted into the wall at right are just two examples. Beaver-cut log ends compliment this home's rustic facade.*

▶ *In this home built for the Lewallen family, the walls are chock-full of burls, cat's-eyes and knobbies, but the focal point is the forked and twisted ridgepost that divides this massive wall of windows. Morton sands all his interior logs and oils them with Columbia Golden Glow every five years. Weatherall western tan chinking is the only kind he'll use since it's stood the test of time, and the tan color won't show stains when re-oiled.*

▲ *In some isolated stands of lodgepole pine, you can find these unusual growths caused by parasitic viruses that attack the tree. More commonly seen in rustic furniture design, Morton uses them throughout his homes as a counterpoint to the otherwise smooth and regular shapes of the logs.*

▶ *Three distinctive shapes and growth patterns commonly found in the woods are built into the kitchen wall of the King home. A crooked limb takes on sculptural qualities after being drawknived, sanded and polished. Below that, the wood is knotted with burls and textured with a large cat's-eye. When hand-worked, each of these configurations exhibit varied and unique colors and patterns in the grain.*

▲ *In a whimsical display of natural form, this limb spans two opposing walls, joining them together in a most unorthodox fashion. While the end result may seem simple, the execution can be quite difficult since positioning the logs is complicated by the corner notches.*

▲ *Huge burled posts set the Rue living room apart at a glance, and provide a pleasing frame for the huge, cut-stone fireplace.*

▶ *Morton has handcrafted around twenty log homes since his start in 1979, and in every one he has tried to incorporate a distinctive, personal touch. The log staircase in the Rue home was one of his trickiest undertakings. Two steps were cut into each log, and the round ends were scribed into the wall. He worked his way around the corner not knowing exactly how, or where, he would end up. According to James, "it was murder!" Except for the fact that the former owner added carpet, he was pleased with the results.*

Scribed to Perfection

Custom log home architecture is the forte of craftsman. The level of care and workmanship is at once visible in the logs, and while many homes purposely communicate their intent via rough-cast trunks, the wood in these walls was treated like fine furniture. Nestled among the trees in Jackson Hole, Wyoming, this fourth-generation home designed by Vince Lee was built in the full-scribe Swedish tradition.

Green cedar logs, felled in the spring as the sap began to run, were peeled with bare hands. Highland Log Builders then carefully scribed and stacked the logs in Canada but, at the owners request, left the bottom two inches of every exposed tree limb in place. Packed in sawdust, the logs arrived at the Wyoming home site where the husband personally trimmed every knob by hand. Swirling grains of wood "like water flowing over rocks in a stream"—were preserved at every point. No less care was given to the finish inside. Some logs were stained and others bleached to create a consistent color. The logs were then varnished to a truly beautiful luster.

▲ *There are a number of different tree species from which to build a home. The one you choose, and the finish you apply, may well set the tone for your design. Here, the grain and color of polished, handpicked, cedar logs envelopes the interiors with rich, yet subtle, warmth.*

▲ *In the gathering room, uncluttered interiors compliment the logs rather than compete with them. Comfort and durability were a priority. Sturdy tapestry fabrics, leather, and a table you can put your feet on should wear beautifully for years. The blue-grey granite in the fireplace is stacked without visible mortar, and is another monument to the achievements of the handcrafter. The fallow deer antler chandelier is from England.*

▶ *Log houses are a family tradition and this is the fourth in a line stretching from Germany to British Columbia. Of those early homes, the one admired most by the owners is built of cedar logs that have weathered to a distinguished silvery grey. Because Wyoming's climate is relatively dry, their own logs will probably get splotchy before anything else, so the owners sped up the process with a stain. Fascia and window trim were matched to the color of the surrounding blue spruce. The osprey that guards the entry is an old Chinese incense pot purchased more than twenty-five years ago.*

◀ *In Swedish cope construction, one green log is carefully scribed to the next. As the wood dries, the logs shrink together for a tighter fit. The logs are back cut in the corners to help facilitate this process. General contractor Robert Ciulla oversaw the log work.*

◀ Logs are, in essence, alive, and newly-cut green logs will shrink several inches over time. In this case, the chinkless Swedish cope method of building is virtually always used, and the home is constructed with major settling in mind. Spaces are left above windows and doors, posts are built on jacks, and stairs are hinged so that the whole building can be lowered as the logs contract. In this home, even the roof is hinged. Here, the stairway is the home's most prominent feature, and space has been allowed for settling at every point of attachment. Finely crafted, the architect likens it to a free-floating wood sculpture.

▼ Wooden yokes are just one example of the trim work that conceal spaces allowed for log settling.

▲ *In this home, the logs are dramatic and impressive, but the owners also wanted to create a separate space that was especially snug and private. In the library, the logs are hidden behind sugar pine paneling. This beautiful, handworked wood, in combination with a Dutch tile fireplace, sets the mood with a comfortable change of pace.*

Medieval Echo

If there is one thing people can do for themselves, it's to feel and trust their likes and dislikes when it comes to designing their own homes. Gerry Spence believes people have lost that sense of self, and he "sees red" when he experiences architects who put their own egos before a client's needs. That was not the case here, and Gerry proudly describes this home as "LaNelle Spence style." His wife, known to most as Imaging, designed their home in its entirety from the land up.

Approaching the house like a native woman might approach a lodging for her family, she first studied the Wyoming site through the seasons, then built and sometimes rebuilt to accommodate their specific needs. At the same time, Imaging incorporated all her dreams and fantasies. As the daughter of a curator of art at the Smithsonian Institute, she travelled extensively with her father visiting every ancient home and castle in Europe. Those childhood memories are reflected here, as are the fascinating old hotels and park lodges of the western United States.

◄ *Designed first on an airplane napkin, then reworked through models constructed from grocery boxes, paper-towel rolls and Lincoln Logs, the Spence house brings to life the imaginings of little girls, and includes a tower, cave, secret passageways and a romantic bedroom about which Gerry jokes, "no husband could possibly live up to!"*

► *This is the fourth house built by the Spences from scratch, but the first in which Gerry turned all the "artist's brushes" over to his wife. From the beginning she had a general footprint worked out in her mind, that included the use of large, chinked logs, slate and huge rocks. She wanted something strong and monumental, and admits she over-built. The house is actually triple-walled construction with framed, super- insulated walls between log siding. Gerry laughs that "you can heat the place with a light bulb." Most of the building materials are old, having been recycled from other places, and people often ask how long the house has been there even though it isn't even finished. The turret (the vertical logs are yet to be finished on the bottom) provides access to the roof in back and a view of the Tetons behind the house. Carefully worked copper flashing and cast-bronze snow clips shaped like eagles, accentuate the level of attention to detail throughout.*

▶ *The owners have collected beautiful, old stained glass doors from England and incorporated them all over the house. Imaging loves antiques—not just because they're old, but because they've been used and have a life and spirit all their own.*

▶ *Imaging thinks that a house should not just reflect who you are but where you've been, and she has a "huge hodgepodge" of furnishings collected from all over the world. Nothing in the house is matched and fitted, and she's not at all shy about mixing African art with American Indian, or Asian pieces with contemporary work. All of the whole logs in the house are balsam spruce averaging thirty-four inches in diameter, and Colorado red stone covers radiant heat floors. Massive boulders are used in two opposing fireplaces in the great room. The home is built on a hill overlooking the mountains and includes a daylight basement with a gym and photography darkroom.*

▲ *The upstairs master bedroom is just beyond Imaging's study in a separate wing that also accesses a mini tower with her private studio (among other things, Imaging is a self-taught fashion designer). In the bedroom, full log gives way to post-and-beam framing. The dark stained logs against a stucco background have a medieval, half-timbered, English Tudor look. The room's center piece, an antique mantle salvaged from an old hotel, followed them from their previous home. Gerry's self-portrait is displayed on the wall above.*

▲ "I've always loved Roman Frescos," says the owner, and this bathroom is fantasy land. Giving her artist-nephew free license to paint the entire room, he came up with many of the same designs that Imaging had admired for years.

◄ *A heavy round-top wooden door off the great room opens to the home's biggest flirt with fancy—a two-story cave that was inspired from a similar room in a Scottish castle. Imaging couldn't shake the image when she returned from her trip and finally came up with a reason to include one in her home. It became an entertainment center for Gerry and their six children. Professionally engineered "surround sound" and a big screen TV almost makes Monday Night football bearable—even for her! Of course, her cats also love the cave and think it was built for them.*

▶ *Since the couple works out of their home, Imaging designed separate office space for both of them. Imaging's study glows with the warmth of brightly painted walls. The wood floors are recycled from waterlogged pine salvaged from the bottom of southeast rivers where they sank many years ago on their way to the mills.*

5 ᵴ POST AND BEAM

In his most enlightening introduction to the book *Wooden Houses,* architectural historian Christian Norberg-Schulz calls the Norwegian stave church "the supreme achievement of wooden architecture." When one considers the monumental accomplishments in this realm of building worldwide, the significance of his statement resounds like a giant fir crashing to earth.

Built in the twelfth and thirteenth centuries, these stave churches exemplified the art of skeletal architecture that later became known as post-and-beam construction. A variation on this theme known as braced or timber frame construction was popularized in Western Europe as timber resources diminished early in the 1600s. As with many things that pass from one culture to another, folk architecture has been hybridized from its beginnings. Today, what many consider post-and-beam architecture is really more akin to timber framed construction. True post-and-beam, or "piece-sur-piece" construction as it is called in Canada, consists of vertical intermediate and corner posts with an infill of round logs or half timbers flattened on two sides.

While French and English fur trappers brought post-and-beam log construction from Canada, the Scandinavian method using notched, horizontal logs prevailed throughout the American frontier. In fact, this style of building has dominated log home design in the United States since its introduction over two hundred years ago. Recently, however, a renewed interest in the more ancient and traditional post-and-beam method of building has arisen.

Post-and-beam systems today can be essentially full-log homes with posted corners, or, more often as is in stave church construction, use logs structurally as posts, girders and roof beams with materials other than logs for infill. This method of building affords tremendous freedom in design. And by posting corners instead of notching them, or by using something other than log infill, less logs are required in building. This is particularly attractive in an age of diminishing natural resources where house logs can be more difficult to obtain.

Along with this facet of construction comes the increasing use of logs for accent—that is incorporating logs into a conventionally built home primarily for aesthetics. So powerful are the design elements inherent in log construction, that well-placed posts, log siding or trim can appease the homeowner who wants to experience logs without actually living in a full log house. Since many of these non-structural accoutrements become part of the post-and-beam design, we have included them here.

▲ *Located in the Black Hills of South Dakota, this stave church is an exact replica of its counterpart in Borgund, Norway. Though hidden from view within the building, the framework of this post-and-beam structure consists, in part, of fifty-two massive Douglas fir logs shipped from Oregon. These logs are used as "staves" or posts and are elaborately carved. This building's sister church in Norway still stands after eight centuries, and there is every reason to believe the "Chapel in the Hills" will endure as well. Photo: Dale A. Jensen*

▶ *Constructed in the traditional post-and-beam or "piece-sur-piece" method, this log house, designed and built by author Art Thiede, uses full round logs as infill between posts. Early American Forest Service and National Park buildings inspired the dark stain and green roof.*

Southwest Post and Beam

An affinity for solid, massive logs and Santa Fe styling was the driving force behind the design of this handsome post-and-beam house. Idaho architect Janet Jarvis effectively combined a variety of building materials and architectural styles to complete the picture for her client, Steve Karakash. Situated on top of a hill, the home's major angles were dictated by the mountain views. As such, it became equally important to locate the primary living areas upstairs. The open kitchen and living rooms are oriented toward one notable peak while the master bedroom faces another. A dumbwaiter was installed to facilitate the transfer of groceries from the garage up to Steve's "reverse living" areas.

◀ *The open design of the house dictated that the utilitarian aspects of the kitchen be downplayed through the careful placements of appliances and handcrafted cabinetry. Jack Burgess created the unique serving island and pedestal table using the natural elements of wood and plaster. The table surfaces are made of alder and black walnut.*

▲ *Deeply recessed rafter bays accentuate the logs over the living room. These bays were created by the addition of structural roofing members over the logs to meet seismic and snow load engineering specifications. The beehive chimney adds to the Santa Fe styling and was built by a violin maker from Wendell, Idaho, who, according to the general contractor Dave Carter, "played his violins as well as he built fireplaces."*

▲ *The judicious use of logs in the context of post-and-beam design is dramatic without being overbearing. Stucco infill between the logs enabled the interplay of Southwest elements in the home's design. A curved "pop out" window on the second floor adds yet another variable and is nicely framed within posts, beams and log accents.*

"Post" Modern in Sun Valley

San Francisco architect Barry Berkus did not let the traditional parameters of log construction interfere with his design for this post-modern residence in Sun Valley, Idaho. While from a distance the log work may seem subtle, closer inspection reveals a different picture. As in the stave church, most of the logs in this structure are used in interior spaces hidden from public view. What isn't hidden however, is the generous use of log accents in the fascia, posting and skirting around the building.

Built on a hill overlooking a golf course, this design accommodates three levels of living space. On entry from the portico, a sculpted pine bridge with glass handrails connects the foyer to a dynamic, formal entertainment core. Walls of glass track the seasons and bathe the rooms in everchanging patterns of light and shadow.

▲ *Though logs are used less frequently in such contemporary designs, they work very well in this home because their rusticity compliments rather than provokes. There are no visible log ends since corner notching is absent. Post-and-beam construction facilitates this building style as does the use of log accents.*

◀ *While the architect could have specified log posts for these railings, he maintains a balance between the masonry and wood by choosing otherwise.*

▶ *The portico leaves no doubt that logs play a very important role in the construction of this home. The abundant use of skylights brings sun under the entry and draws attention to the extensive truss work overhead.*

◀ *Using massive logs for these posts and setting them on large pedestals gives a Greek Revival impression. Log siding on the fascia is mitered at the corners for a clean, trim look.*

▲ *As with many contemporary designs, the kitchen is open and incorporates a comfortable informal sitting area where family and guests can mingle. With floor-to-ceiling windows admitting light, and white plaster walls reflecting it, there is no lack of natural illumination.*

◄ *An amalgam of building materials contributes to the contemporary feel of this home's interior spaces. Here the architect combines polished marble at the fireplace with a sandstone hearth, while log posts and rafters are juxtaposed with fir beams and concrete columns.*

A River Runs Through

If ever there was a home and setting so complimentary as to be inseparable, this would have to be it. Located near the majestic Teton mountain range in western Wyoming, this residence draws much of its grandeur and charm from the nearby park lodges in Yellowstone and Teton National Parks.

While this house takes on a traditional post-and-beam appearance, all the horizontal and vertical log surfaces are milled logs sandwiched to conventional framing. Apart from structural posts, much of the log work is purely for aesthetics. Although this style of building is more expensive, there are certain advantages. Initially, all construction can take place on site, and any settling problems are essentially eliminated. Finally, and most importantly for the owners, this system is exceedingly energy efficient.

▶ *In the framing detail around the door, large half logs set themselves apart from the wall.*

▲ *In the living room, the owners' period furnishings co-exist with the rustic look of log posts and beams. An overhanging balcony serves as the family room upstairs and brings the ceiling down for a more intimate feel in a portion of the great room below. The rest of the area remains open to accommodate a grand pipe organ and majestic views.*

▲ *Attention to detail is evident throughout the house from the use of naturally curved railings to the dentil moldings on the fascia. The design results from the combined efforts of the owners and designer Ellis Nunn.*

◀ *The barn, unlike the main house, is constructed from full-round logs with saddle-notched corners. Carefully scribed strips of wood replace synthetic chinking in tribute to an authentic regional tradition.*

▼ *This home's dark stained logs are balanced by the lighter colored slate roof and generous use of river rock. As pointed out later in the chapter on maintenance, such heavily pigmented stains also afford greater protection to the logs.*

Paul Bunyan Architecture

Surrounded by towering Jeffrey pines and granite boulders, this stunning residence sits on the shoreline of Lake Tahoe, California. Designed for Art and Veronica Engel by Dale Munsterman of nearby Carnelian Bay, the house combines log post-and-beam and conventional framing with an unconventional bit of log work in the building's gable ends.

True to the dictum of "form follows function," the inspiration for this crisscross truss design came from engineering requirements to provide shear resistance for the walls. This permitted the use of expansive areas of glass that have little or no structural value.

As this designer's first foray into log construction, the challenges were formidable for both he and general contractor, Lakeshore Builders. Since construction didn't begin until early fall, it took considerable effort to get the building enclosed before heavy winter snows set in. As soon as the log package came down from Custom Log Homes in Montana, two large cranes and fifteen men set about the three-week task of reassembling the structure. With what seemed to be a forest of giant logs in place, the crew laughingly termed the design "Paul Bunyan" architecture.

▲ *Encouraged by the owners to take creative license, the designer and builders outdid themselves. As the first structure of its kind in the high Sierra, this novel home has quickly become a landmark.*

All "Paul Bunyan" photos: Bob Brown

▶ *One of the attributes of post-and-beam construction is the ability to use various materials for infill between logs. This feature is well displayed in the front of this house. Here the design incorporates a combination of river rock, glass, cedar clapboards and stucco—a virtual palette of building materials. A hand-carved bear sharpens its claws on the tree just left of the entry.*

▶ *Interior designer Sandra York worked around the owners' existing furnishings to create informal spaces with a slight western bent. In winter, the living room becomes the central focus of the home with its huge river-rock fireplace. Summertime activity, however, brings a shift to the outdoors and the glorious lake.*

◄ *In the hallway, visible interplay of posts, girders, and rafters reveal all the basic elements of post-and-beam design.*

▶ *A handcrafted front door by Timeless Sculptures in Kings Beach, California, is a powerful element in this well-orchestrated entrance.*

▲ *Twig work cabinetry and handmade tiles featuring forest plants and animals build on an outdoor motif. Breakfast is served at a kitchen table set into a bay overlooking the lake.*

▲ *Huge, four-hundred-year-old larch logs provide appropriate scale for this cedar-sided home in its imposing mountain environment. Soaring, passive solar walls of windows, permitted by the open character of post-and-beam construction, utilize the most energy efficient heat mirror glass available when the house was built by Jack Wilkie Builders in*

woods," he and architect Steven Conger spent literally hundreds of hours over a period of years before a very different floor plan finally emerged. In the end, this forty-one hundred square-foot home evokes remembrance of many architectural motifs ranging from park lodges and the Adirondack Great Camps to Greek temples and Japanese Shinto shrines.

◀ *Like the mountains breaking from the valley plane, numerous dormers create a diversion from the horizontal roof line. They also open up space in the interior and flood the area with afternoon light.*

Land Before Place

The building of a custom home can take many forms. There are a myriad of architectural designs, building materials, structural compositions and spatial arrangements from which to choose. Add to this the diversity of outdoor environments, and the combinations are endless. Still, no matter how many paths ultimately exist, they all start from one place—the land on which the building sits.

For many people, a building site may be nothing more than a quarter-acre lot in some suburban subdivision. For owner Richard Lewis it was something much more. Situated a few miles from the chic ski resort town of Aspen, Colorado, this thirty-seven-acre site had been purchased some ten years before building began. In those ensuing years, Richard both camped and skied on the land—exploring it intimately and watching it change through cycles of the sun and seasons. First envisioning a "little log cabin in the

▼ *Rough-hewn larch contrasts with the more refined look of sawn cedar siding and divided light windows. Spruce blue trim, carried throughout the design, forms a subtle union to the surrounding forest.*

▲ *The kitchen, a few steps up and overlooking the great room, is set apart by its curving breakfast bar. The countertop is built from ancient cypress deadwood that Richard discovered in a unusual commune tucked away in the California desert. Grey flagstone floors hide a network of radiant-heat pipes that provide an even warmth to the home.*

► *Among this home's most striking features is the log pergola over the spa. This exposed extension of log posts and beams echoes the skeletal framework constituting the main house. Because it was so beautiful in its simplicity, the architect wanted to showcase it outside, even though special care would be necessary to protect the logs from weather.*

◀ *While many "log" houses tend to look rustic on the exterior, their interiors will often reflect other styles. Here, however, in contrast to the simple, clean lines outside, large rough-cut granite boulders are used in the central stone fireplace and chimney that dominates within. Log furniture and rich kilim textiles combine with a profusion of greenery for a very earthy look. A stream, channeled off a creek flowing behind the house, actually runs inside under the stairs and around the perimeter of the living room. It exits again at the front and empties into the rock-lined, artificial pond.*

▶ *The entire upstairs is open to the great room below and basically consists of one big "H" shaped master suite. The sleeping loft and master bath take up one side, while a combined office/ exercise space and huge walk-in closet are located opposite. A bridge above the living area connects the two spaces. This beautiful bed is built of red cedar and imported from Mexico.*

▲ *Inspired by a 1930s ranch house in Grand Teton National Park, Doug and Lee began piecing together large, octagonal spaces and pop-out bays. A tricky plan to design and build, this multi-faceted home was made feasible by the use of posted corners.*

▶ *Lee spends countless hours cultivating plants in her expansive greenhouse, and tending wild flowers in the gardens around their home. Here, native lupine and daisies burst through the greens of summer in a vivid display.*

Post and Beam—One Log at a Time

One advantage of post-and-beam construction is that it works well as an on-site method of building. Today, the log shells of most handcrafted homes are pre-built in company log yards. While this method has many benefits, it leaves the owners out of the building process. Doug Walton and Lee Whiting of Hailey, Idaho, were not about to stand on the sidelines and watch somebody else build their home.

Though Doug had little previous log construction experience, he was not daunted by the complexity of his structure. Post and beam affords a great amount of latitude in design, and this home uses that to its advantage to include twenty-seven roof planes on a series of circular bays.

▲ *The owner built his front door with strips of vertical grain fir through-bolted together. Local wood sculptor Larry Lefner did the carvings from a picture on a postcard. The Chinese characters are proverbs blessing the home and those who enter.*

◀ *Lodgepole pine logs were bought in a Forest Service sale and harvested by the owner. They were then laid up on the building using a "gin pole" designed and built by Walton. The pole, (at building's center) which uses a motorized boom, was moved up to the second floor as the building grew in height.*

▲ The scaffolding was still in place when Larry and the owners conferred that the log ends overhead needed some attention. Doug says "that's when Larry scampered on up and whacked out the designs" pictured here.

◄ Post-and-beam construction was not just relegated to this home's exterior but was carried inside to support the floor systems as well. Most of the logs were left in their naturally weathered condition, and character logs, like the huge burled post at the kitchen counter, were used freely throughout.

▶ *The Walton home, like those we have loosely defined as craftsman-styled, is touched by the liberating forms of nature and the artisan's hand. The owner's friend, Larry Lefner, also crafted the newel post at the base of the stairs. Carved from spruce, it suggests two lovers embracing. Doug found the walking sticks in the forest.*

BIBLIOGRAPHY

Kaiser, Harvey H. *Great Camps of the Adirondacks.* Boston: David R. Godine Publisher Inc., 1982.

Kirschenbaum, Howard. *The Story of Sagamore.* Raquette Lake, NY: Sagamore Institute, 1990.

Lewis, Scott. *The Rainforest Book, How You Can Save the World's Rainforests.* Venice, CA: The Living Planet Press, 1990.

Mack, Daniel. *Making Rustic Furniture.* New York: Sterling/Lark Publishing Co. Inc., 1992.

McRaven, Charles. *Building the Hewn Log House.* New York: Thomas Y. Crowell, Publishers, 1978.

———. *Building with Stone.* Pownal, VT: Garden Way Publishing, 1989.

———. *Country Blacksmithing.* New York: Harper & Row, 1981.

———. *Dog Trots and Saddlebags: Building and Restoring the Hewn Log House.* Cincinnati: F & W Publications, 1994.

Mix Foley, Mary. *The American House.* New York: Harper Colophon Books, Harper and Row Publishers, 1980.

Opolovnikov, Alexander and Y. Opolovnikov. *The Wooden Architecture of Russia, Houses, Fortifications, Churches.* New York: Harry N. Abrams Inc. Publishers, 1989.

Pearson, David. *The Natural House Book.* New York: Fireside Book, Simon & Schuster, Inc., 1989.

Zuckerman, Seth. *Saving Our Ancient Forests.* Venice, CA: The Living Planet Press, 1991.

ENDANGERED AND OLD-GROWTH SPECIES

PLEASE AVOID USING ENDANGERED TROPICAL HARDWOODS AND OLD-GROWTH SPECIES—

North America has been blessed with an abundance of forest lands that have supplied wood products since early settlers first felled trees to build their cabins. Today, however, timber cutting on many National Forests exceeds sustainable harvest. Biologically diverse old-growth woodlands are being rapidly depleted, and ongoing pollution and acid rain is damaging and killing large tracts of forest throughout the developed world. On a global scale, tropical rainforests are being destroyed at an alarming rate, which in turn, threatens the health and security of our entire planet.

While the log home industry consumes a fraction of our timber resources, the amount of wood used in a single log structure would easily build two or more conventionally framed homes of the same size. Therefore, it is the responsibility of every log home designer, builder and buyer to support sustainable forest management practices, and avoid buying or using endangered tropical hardwoods and vanishing indigenous old-growth species.

On the following page, we have listed some of the major organizations dedicated to preserving these vitally important tropical and old-growth environments. They need your support, and we encourage you to contact them for current information on any tree species in question.

Thank you.

ENDANGERED AND OLD-GROWTH SPECIES

Please Contact the Following Organizations for More Information:

Association of Forest Service Employees for Environmental Ethics
P.O. Box 11615
Eugene, OR 97440.
(503)484-2692
Old-Growth

Conservation International
1015 18th St., NW, Suite 1002
Washington, DC 20036
Rainforests

Global Tomorrow Coalition
1325 G St., NW, Suite 915
Washington, DC 20005
Rainforests

Natural Resources Defense Council
40 W. 20th St.
New York, NY 10011
(212)727-2700
Rainforests and Old-Growth

Rainforest Action Network
301 Broadway, Suite A
San Francisco, CA 94133
Rainforests

The Wilderness Society
900 17th St. NW
Washington, DC 20006-2596
(202)833-2300
Old- Growth—national organization and addresses for state groups in CA, OR, WA and SE Alaska

World Wildlife Fund/Conservation Foundation
1250 24th St. NW
Washington, DC 20037
Rainforests

Zero Population Growth Inc.
1400 10th St., NW, Suite 320
Washington, DC 20036
Rainforests

Maintenance and Technical Notes

With Architectural Illustrations By: Bill Ransom

This book is obviously not a technical journal intended to guide the professional or amateur builder/designer through the intricacies of logbuilding. It will, however, inspire many people to build, or have built, a home of logs. Since this is such a unique and often misunderstood approach to building, the authors felt a responsibility to explain, at least on a fundamental level, the differences, alternatives, problems and solutions peculiar to log construction.

The information for this chapter was derived from personal construction experiences. Additionally, much knowledge was acquired through visiting hundreds of log homes and interviewing their architects, builders and owners. Many written resources were also consulted and are listed in the bibliography following the chapter. While the subject of log home design, construction and preservation is too complex to cover in one chapter, we have tried to present, mostly in simple terms and illustrations, the most common situations relating to these topics.

Log Home Maintenance

Wood Preservation

At one time or another, we have all seen, in real life or in pictures, examples of old log cabins that seemed one good push away from collapse. Abandoned and neglected, many of these early relics eventually decayed their way back to the earth that nurtured their existence. While this may be poetic justice at its finest, it's a fate that modern-day log home owners want to avoid. With adequate wood care and preventative maintenance, the log homes built today will endure for centuries.

Increasing the longevity of wood in a structure involves protecting it from the destructive forces of nature. This can be accomplished both from design and maintenance perspectives. Since design considerations are discussed elsewhere, our focus here will be on preservation through preventative maintenance.

Without delving into the cellular structure and chemical make up of the tree, suffice it to say that most woods contain naturally occurring oils that resist weathering and decay. Deterioration occurs over time as these oils are leached from the wood and need to be replaced. What they are replaced with, and how, forms the basis of wood preservation.

To solve or prevent log degradation, you must first pinpoint the problem and its source. For example, a log house subject to a hot, dry southwestern climate, will need a different formulation of log preservative than its counterpart in the Smoky Mountains of Tennessee, where excessive moisture enhances the growth of decay bacteria. Not only will the formulation be different, but the log preparation and application of preservative may also differ. And while regional climates may dictate general preservation techniques, cases of crossover also occur. For instance, the house in the arid Southwest might have irrigation sprinklers wetting the lower courses of logs and subjecting them to decay, while upper courses are dried and weathered by ultra-violet and infrared sunlight. —A note about lawn sprinklers: it's our contention that malfunctioning and misdirected sprinkler heads account for a significant portion of log decay problems.

Once the source of decay has been identified, there are a plethora of wood preservatives on the market from which to choose, each claiming to be the best that modern technology and chemistry can produce. So how do you know which to choose? How important are the differences? What is their toxicity, cost and ease of application over new or old wood? Specific questions like these can only be answered by consulting with professionals or reading a profusion of associated literature. Since it is beyond the scope of this chapter to analyze every product or every situation in need of attention, we will focus on important points that will generally apply.

1. While this first point has little to do with preservatives, it has everything to do with wood preservation. Prevent water from coming into contact with your logs! Lawn sprinkler heads, roof drip splash back, inadequate roof overhangs, leaking gutters, snow buildup and improper flashing techniques are just a few areas of concern. Of the three ingredients necessary for decay fungi to flourish (oxygen, heat and water), water is really the only element that can be effectively controlled.

2. Inspect your logs carefully to pinpoint potentially damaging conditions. If the logs are unusually moist and have fungal stains on them, the first step is to identify and eliminate the source of excessive moisture. Logs must be thoroughly cleansed with a solution of soap and bleach. After cleaning, the wood should dry completely, and a preservative solution containing a water repellent and mildewcide needs to be applied. By reapplying this solution until the logs will no longer accept any more preservative, you insure a lasting treatment. If, on the other hand, you find the logs on the west and south side of your structure to be so dry that the surface of the wood disintegrates when you scratch it, you must select a preservative that contains oils, possibly pigments, and ultra violet blockers to retard this disintegration. Following are some important points relating to solution application:

a. Before applying any solution to the logs, make sure the logs are clean of dirt, fungi and the accumulation of previous preservatives before applying any solution. This can be accomplished by hand scrubbing, pressure washing, or, in extreme cases, sandblasting.

b. Dry wood will ensure maximum absorption of preservative material, so give the logs plenty of time to dry. If this is not possible (i.e. either the logs are still "green" or exist in an extremely wet environment, etc.), use a preservative that will diffuse under moist conditions such as the newly available borate solutions.

c. Put as much material on the logs as they will absorb, but don't try to get it all on in one application. Apply several coats over several days for more lasting protection. The use of low pressure agricultural sprayers followed by hand brushing works well.

d. Don't apply an impermeable finish such as varnish or paint to the exterior surface of the logs. This will trap moisture within the log and can lead to finish failure and log decay.

e. Incorporate a regular program of preventative maintenance on your logs. Don't walk away from your home after one treatment thinking you have everlasting protection.

3. Caulk all upper surface checks on the exterior of logs (see *Illustration 1*). This may seem like an overwhelming task at first, given the number of logs in a home, but if the structure was built properly in the first place, most of the logs will have been placed on the wall with the largest checks facing down and self-draining. The authors, who specialize in log home preservation, restoration and weatherization, have found that this detail has been overlooked far too long. Rain and snow that accumulates in exposed checks (splits or cracks which occur as wood dries) creates mini-reservoirs of water that begin the decay process deep within the wood. While caulking can be time consuming , benefits are far reaching and include better thermal efficiency, log preservation and insect control.

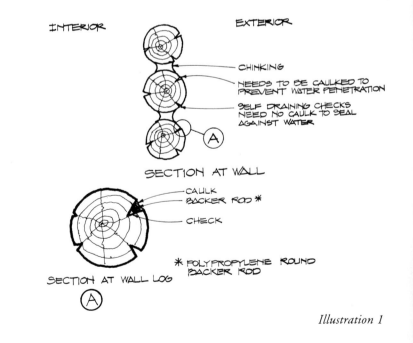

Illustration 1

Thermal Efficiencies and Deficiencies of Log Homes

If you own a log home, especially one built with large diameter logs (ten or more inches in diameter), you are probably aware of one of the greatest benefits of log home living. That is, the home seems warmer in winter and cooler in summer than conventionally built structures with framed walls and cavity insulation. This is not an illusion, but sound fact based on the premise that the more mass you have in a structure, the less pronounced the temperature swings are within its confines. Put another way, as the outside temperature drops, the inside of the building tends to retain its warmth as the logs release heat stored within their mass. Conversely, in the summer the log home interior will remain cooler. As outside temperatures climb, the mass of the logs, which are now relatively cool compared to rising air temperatures, prevent overheating.

All of this, however, can be short circuited by one very important inherent weakness in log homes, especially in full round, handcrafted structures. That weakness is air infiltration, and it can originate from several sources. As the logs lose their moisture, they will shrink. Corner notches that were once tight, now open up, and lateral checks (see *Illustration 2*) can penetrate directly into the interior of the house through log ends. These same penetrating checks can also substantially decrease the insulative value of a log. Sometimes incorrect or inadequate insulation around window and door openings will permit air penetration as the building moves and settles. In scribed log houses (see *Illustration 3*), the shoulders of the lateral grooves can open up from log movement permitting leakage at these points. This infiltration can be difficult to pinpoint since air will travel along the lateral groove and exit at a point far removed from its source.

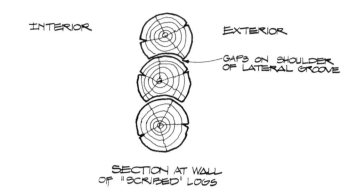

SECTION AT WALL
OF "SCRIBED" LOGS

Illustration 3

If your log home is in a cold climate, as many of them are, significant air infiltration is unacceptable. It is the duty of the architect to address this issue and incorporate mitigating factors into the design. There are many excellent products on the market and proven weatherization techniques that, if implemented, will render air infiltration obsolete. It is then the responsibility of the builder to ensure that the appropriate steps are executed throughout the building while keeping in mind that log shrinkage will cause movement at some point in time. Final responsibility, however, rests with the owner since it will take several years for the logs to finally reach equilibrium with their environment. It is at this point that final sealing of the structure can take place, and any remaining drafts can be effectively sealed off with caulk.

Insect Control

It seems that while log homes are attractive to people wanting a return to more traditional building styles, they are also attractive to insects. One of the most effective advertisements we have seen, pictures three of the most common and destructive wood boring insects known to exist—a powder post beetle, termite and carpenter ant. Above the picture, in bold print, are the words, "You aren't the only one who's anxious to move into your new home." You guessed it, the ad is for a wood preservative.

Scare tactics aside, insects, benign or otherwise, can be a real problem in log homes. We can remember all too well sitting in our sun room several years ago and watching the hatch take place. It was still winter outside, but the temperature in this particular room was warm enough to hatch a bevy of flying critters from house flies to yellow jackets. We could hardly believe our eyes and began to wonder if having a log home would mean sharing the premises with these pests. Sure, we could fumigate every six

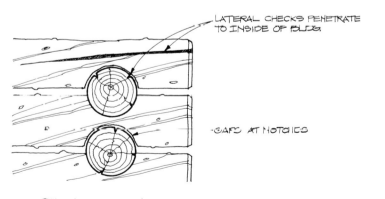

SHRINKAGE AT NOTCHES

Illustration 2

months or so, but the prospect of living with toxic chemicals seemed even less appealing. Instead, we began to experiment by caulking checks where insects sought refuge and laid their eggs. That is when we realized that by sealing our logs, we accomplished two things. We denied the insects a place to breed and also sealed our house to air infiltration. Using this process, we were able to eliminate upwards of 90 percent of these pests and have since for numerous other home owners.

While this may take care of non-wood boring insects, the borers are another matter. In many cases, insects like the powder post beetle are in the logs before the logs are in the home. Carpenter ants can also come in with the wood, though that is a less frequent occurrence. Treatment for these damaging types of insects usually involves strong insecticides that are best applied by professional exterminating contractors. In the case of termites, both the wood and the ground surrounding the structure have to be treated. It is worth mentioning here that if the logs are treated at the factory with insecticides, fungicides, mildewcides and other preserving chemicals, they will be less prone to damage from decay, bacteria and insects. However, the full-round, hand-peeled logs used in most custom homes are rarely treated in this manner. Not only would it be cost prohibitive, but it is usually unnecessary.

Chinking

One thing that revolutionized custom log home building was the development of synthetic chinking compounds. Once the "Achilles' heel" of log home construction, acrylic latex chinking is a far more effective product than its cement-based predecessor. While mortar is still used on occasion, especially in hewn-log restorations, the new chinking compounds are far superior. Excellent adhesion and elasticity helps form a tight bond to the wood and accommodate log shrinkage. With mortar, the logs generally shrink away, permitting water and air to penetrate the joint. *(see Illustration 4).* In the past, chinking, which was the weakest point of the wall with regard to thermal efficiency, now is the strongest, surpassing even the logs themselves in resistance to thermal conductivity *(see Illustration 5).* Expanded color choices have also been a boon to homeowners and designers, since chinking is a prominent part of the overall appearance of a home. Another separate and distinct style of chinking that has found its own niche among log home enthusiasts is the use of scribed wood strips or poles between the logs *(see Illustration 6).* This traditional chink style was especially prevalent in Jackson Hole, Wyoming, and still is. It is a labor-intensive process that takes a skilled craftsman to execute properly, but for some, the regional authenticity is worth the extra cost.

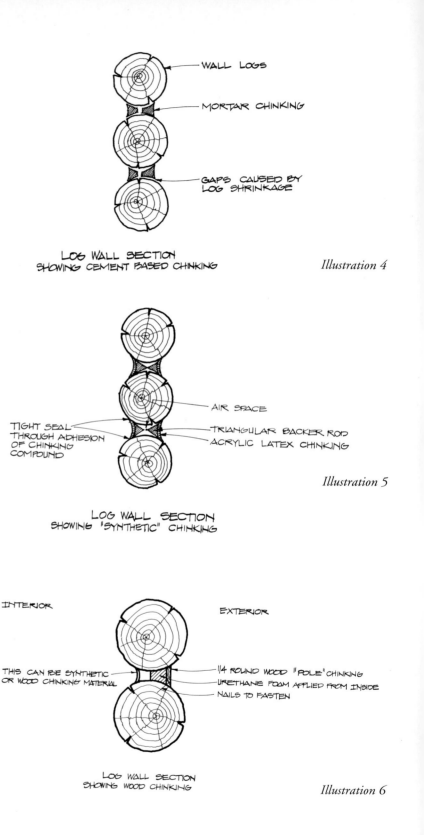

LOG WALL SECTION
SHOWING CEMENT BASED CHINKING

Illustration 4

LOG WALL SECTION
SHOWING "SYNTHETIC" CHINKING

Illustration 5

LOG WALL SECTION
SHOWING WOOD CHINKING

Illustration 6

DESIGN CRITERIA

Over the past ten years, the log home industry has matured in an extraordinary manner. The quality and quantity of log homes has never been greater, and innovative designs and fine craftsmanship have created a renaissance unequaled since the days of the Great Camps of the Adirondacks. Even *Architectural Digest,* the preeminent publication on architectural diversity, routinely showcases log homes, while in the past, such houses rarely graced their pages. What has fueled the revival of this construction form that was once confined to summer cabins and hunting camps? There are many reasons, but among the most influential has been the involvement of architects and other professionals in the design process. Because of this involvement, many of the log homes built today are on the cutting edge of design and engineering technology. They are stronger, more energy efficient and architecturally diverse. In the following sections we will look at some of these new technologies in combination with the time-honored craft of log building itself.

Foundations

There was a time when all you had to do was place some flat stones on the ground and start laying your logs up. Of course, today most foundations consist of poured concrete footings and walls. This method works for log homes as well, with some modifications. Since log walls and posts are considerably heavier than their frame counterparts, it is often wise to increase the size of the footings where the logs will lay. This may be more important in marginally load bearing soils. However, since building codes often call for over-engineered foundations to begin with, problems probably won't arise except in unusual situations where the design dictates overly tall walls or excessive point-loading from posts.

Roof Structures

The options for roof design are numerous and could alone fill a book . We will address the most common designs applicable to log homes.

1. Roofs with log purlins laid parallel to the ridge log (see *Illustration 7*) are among the most popular in log home design. Not only is it the least costly roof system that still employs logs in the structure, but it will tolerate settling better than a raftered roof. The drawbacks to this design are the number of interior posts or bearing walls that are required to support the purlins. The use of trusses or multiple purlins, can reduce the number of supporting members, but not without escalating your costs.

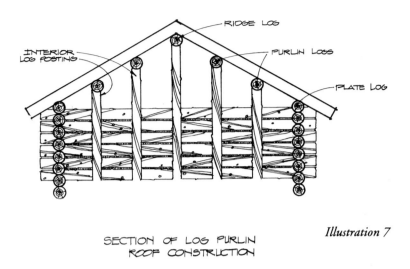

SECTION OF LOG PURLIN ROOF CONSTRUCTION

Illustration 7

2. Raftered roofs, with logs running perpendicular to the ridge (see *Illustration 8*), are more traditional, partly because rafters are usually of shorter length and smaller girth than purlins and therefore easier to get up on the roof. (Cranes were in short supply fifty to one hundred years ago.) In a full-log gable (see *Illustration 9*), however, a raftered roof can present problems due to the differential in settling between the ridge log and plate log. If the rafter is attached at these two members (which it usually is), outward thrust can displace the plate logs on the wall. This can be prevented by the use of collar ties on the rafters or with floor joists spanning the affected walls (see *Illustration 10*).

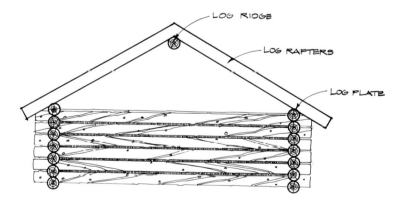

SECTION OF LOG RAFTER CONSTRUCTION

Illustration 8

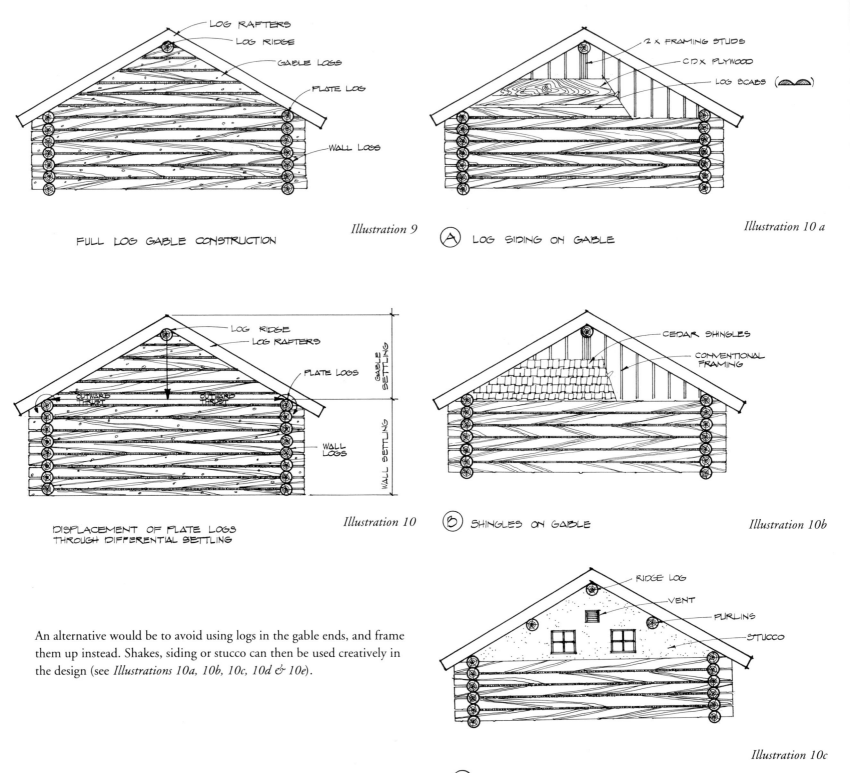

FULL LOG GABLE CONSTRUCTION

LOG RAFTERS
LOG RIDGE
GABLE LOGS
PLATE LOG
WALL LOGS

Illustration 9

Ⓐ LOG SIDING ON GABLE

2 X FRAMING STUDS
CDX PLYWOOD
LOG SCABS

Illustration 10 a

DISPLACEMENT OF PLATE LOGS
THROUGH DIFFERENTIAL SETTLING

LOG RIDGE
LOG RAFTERS
PLATE LOGS
GABLE SETTLING
WALL SETTLING
OUTWARD THRUST
OUTWARD THRUST
WALL LOGS

Illustration 10

Ⓑ SHINGLES ON GABLE

CEDAR SHINGLES
CONVENTIONAL FRAMING

Illustration 10b

An alternative would be to avoid using logs in the gable ends, and frame them up instead. Shakes, siding or stucco can then be used creatively in the design (see *Illustrations 10a, 10b, 10c, 10d & 10e*).

Ⓒ STUCCO GABLE END

RIDGE LOG
VENT
PURLINS
STUCCO

Illustration 10c

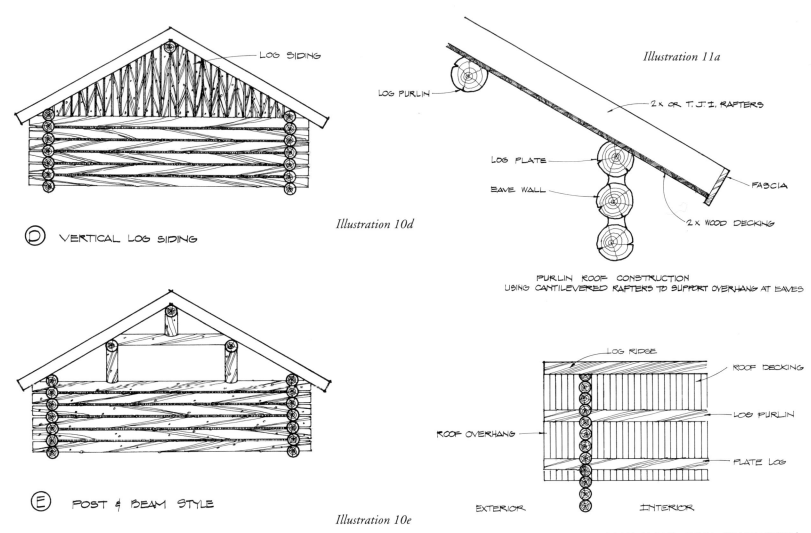

LOG SIDING

Illustration 10d

Ⓓ VERTICAL LOG SIDING

Ⓔ POST & BEAM STYLE

Illustration 10e

LOG PURLIN

2 X OR T.J.I. RAFTERS

LOG PLATE

EAVE WALL

FASCIA

2 X WOOD DECKING

PURLIN ROOF CONSTRUCTION
USING CANTILEVERED RAFTERS TO SUPPORT OVERHANG AT EAVES

Illustration 11a

LOG RIDGE

ROOF DECKING

ROOF OVERHANG

LOG PURLIN

PLATE LOG

EXTERIOR

INTERIOR

GABLE OVERHANG WITH PURLIN CONSTRUCTION

Illustration 11b

Another possibility involves detailing the rafters with a slip joint at the plate log. While easier with dimensioned lumber, this option can be a tricky maneuver with log rafters since structural integrity may be compromised. Having said that, if you are determined to build full log gables, select your driest logs at this point in construction to assure a minimum of shrinkage and settling. Before moving into another area of roof design, it might be worthwhile to make one more point. In a purlined roof, the rake overhang is supported by the cantilevered purlins past the wall—an easy detail to build. On the other hand, there is no structural support at the eaves for any overhang, and reinforcement must then be supplied by the addition of rafters (see *Illustration 11a*) over the purlins (see *Illustration 11b*). This is not usually a problem since some sort of insulation space is needed anyway.

With a raftered roof the rake overhang must be supported by a truss or rafter, however, there is adequate support here for the eave overhangs utilizing the rafter tails. In conventional construction using dimensioned rafter material or trusses, these situations are not a problem because the framing materials can be hidden with fascia and soffits. However, in log construction where it is desirable to expose log framing material, the roof factors discussed here need to be considered. Many times it is more expedient and cost effective to dimensionally frame the roof on a log house, and then add false purlins, rafter tails and other log "accents" later (see *Illustration 12*).

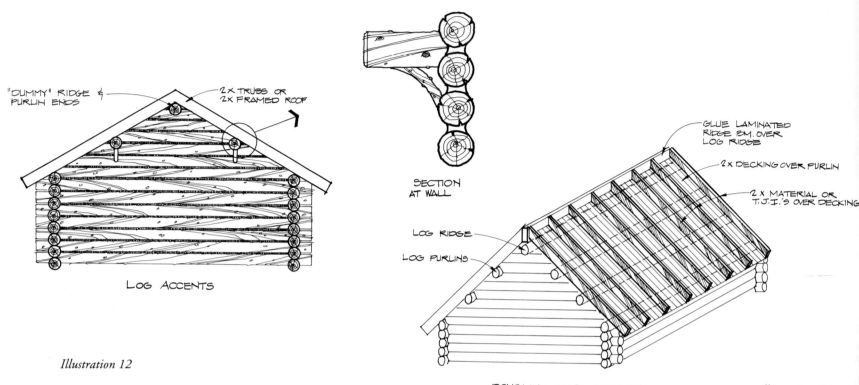

"DUMMY" RIDGE &
PURLIN ENDS

2X TRUSS OR
2X FRAMED ROOF

LOG ACCENTS

Illustration 12

SECTION
AT WALL

GLUE LAMINATED
RIDGE BM. OVER
LOG RIDGE

2X DECKING OVER PURLIN

2X MATERIAL OR
T.J.I.'S OVER DECKING

LOG RIDGE

LOG PURLINS

DOUBLED ROOF FRAMING

Illustration 13

3. Other roofing options could include timber framing, which may embody rafter, purlin, truss design, or some combination. The only real difference between a log roof and one of timbers is the use of dimensioned lumber. This is a big difference, however, when it comes to fabricating the structure. The consistency of sawn lumber makes its much easier to lay out and cut the roof, especially more complex designs. It also results in a stronger structure that will "pencil out" better in engineering calculations. In my experience as a builder, as log homes become bigger and more complex, the required engineering almost makes the logs in the roof structurally superfluous, especially in seismic and heavy snow load areas. You usually end up with two separate roof frames—one structural and the other incorporating logs for aesthetics (see *Illustration 13*).

4. Other options for roof design entail the use of nominal two-inch framing lumber or trusses. If structural elements need to be visible in this kind of roof design, they could be added later as previously mentioned. Non-structural logs could then be placed aesthetically in high-profile areas of the house such as the entry or living room. This would be a cost effective approach to log roof design, and, when properly done, is nearly indistinguishable from the real thing.

5. There is one more area of roof design that is worth mentioning because of the associated problems of decay. By extending purlins and even rafters past the overhangs, you will expose the wood to the destructive forces of weather. Unless considerable effort is taken to protect or maintain these exposed tails, they will eventually decay. Celebrate log roof structure, but don't flaunt it with bad design.

Log Shrinkage

As interest in log home construction rekindled itself in the 1970s, little attention was given to the effects of log shrinkage and the attendant problem of wall settling (see *Illustration 14*). While green-log construction took some shrinkage into account, so called "dry" log construction often overlooked the fact that these logs would also settle (some more than others depending on the moisture content of the wood). It seemed as though builders and designers were either ignoring the problem or unaware of its consequences. As a result, many log homes were built (and some still are) that have suffered from this deficiency in design.

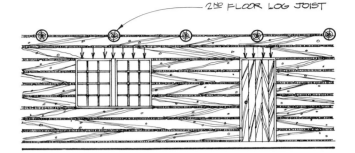

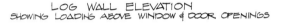

LOG WALL ELEVATION
SHOWING LOADING ABOVE WINDOW & DOOR OPENINGS

Illustration 15

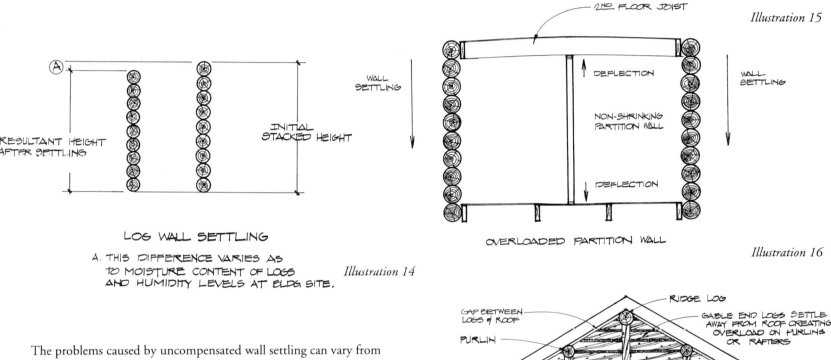

RESULTANT HEIGHT AFTER SETTLING

INITIAL STACKED HEIGHT

WALL SETTLING

LOG WALL SETTLING

A. THIS DIFFERENCE VARIES AS TO MOISTURE CONTENT OF LOGS AND HUMIDITY LEVELS AT BLDG. SITE.

Illustration 14

DEFLECTION

NON-SHRINKING PARTITION WALL

DEFLECTION

WALL SETTLING

OVERLOADED PARTITION WALL

Illustration 16

The problems caused by uncompensated wall settling can vary from relatively harmless dry wall cracking to more serious structural failures. Excessive loading can pinch doors and windows (see *Illustration 15*). Framed walls, not designed to be load bearing, can distort and overload floor and ceiling joist systems with dire consequences (see *Illustration 16*). Gable end log walls can settle away from the roof causing it to "float" and create excessive forces on posts and purlins (see *Illustration 17*).

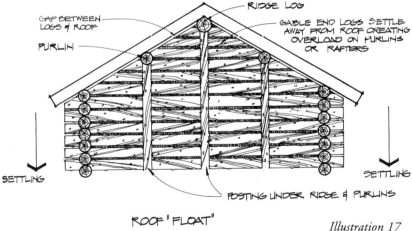

ROOF "FLOAT"

Illustration 17

With large diameter logs, most shrinkage occurs one or two heating seasons after the building is finished. How, then, does the homeowner become aware of these problems? It will usually be quite obvious as the symptoms mentioned above manifest themselves. Besides the previously mentioned dry wall cracking, there can also be cracking in the tile work, especially in second floor bathrooms. Windows and doors will begin sticking, and overloaded framed partition walls will "punch" through ceiling drywall or deflect finished flooring materials. Sometimes deflections in purlins or log joists can be seen as they pass over posts and walls.

With such significant consequences, how do we effect the cure? Can a log house be built that will move while still maintaining structural integrity? The answer, of course, is yes, but it takes a conscious awareness and commitment from both the builder and designer.

Since log walls settle around nonshrinking members of the structure, (i.e. posts, framed walls, masonry, etc.) it is necessary to create "settling spaces" around these components and to incorporate an adjusting device that will take up this movement. These adjustable connectors must be designed to provide adequate bearing and uplift resistance, and still be readily accessible (see *Illustration 18*).

How much room to leave for settling is always a bit of a dilemma because one wants to leave enough without being excessive. A general rule of thumb is roughly ¾" per foot of "green" log wall and ⅛" per foot of logs believed to have a moisture content of less than 15 percent. This could be more or less, of course, depending on the wood and the average humidity levels that exist at the building site. If necessary, specific measurements of the wood can be taken with moisture meters. Building with "green" logs usually dictates a chinkless, scribed method of construction, but remember that chinked homes built with seasoned wood may also require settling provisions.

The mechanical devices described above offer the greatest precision and flexibility when confronting settling, however there are simpler and more direct ways to deal with the problem. While not as effective, they may be viable alternatives, especially for less complex structures and leaner building budgets.

One method entails the use of shims under posts. Using several thicknesses of spacing material will permit the lowering of posts as the building settles. It is important to provide "jack points" (see *Illustration 19*) so that these posts can be lifted and the shims removed. Once all movement has been accounted for, posts can be securely anchored to their bases. A second option is to build out of level to anticipate settling (see *Illustration 20*). This is the least desirable way to compensate for log shrinkage, but it is better than doing nothing.

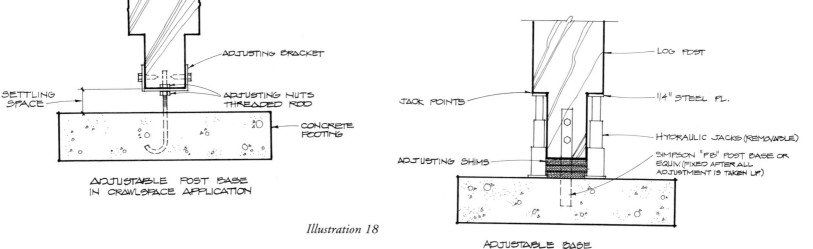

ADJUSTABLE POST BASE
IN CRAWLSPACE APPLICATION

Illustration 18

ADJUSTABLE BASE
USING SHIMS

Illustration 19

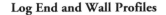

FLOOR BEAM
LOG JOIST

AFTER SETTLING
POSITION

POST
(NON ADJUSTABLE)

SETTLING

SETTLING

BUILDING OUT OF LEVEL

Illustration 20

Log Species

While many species of wood have been used successfully in log homes, the number of species used by commercial log building companies is actually quite limited. In the western United States, softwoods including firs, (Douglas, white and red), pines, (lodgepole, ponderosa, etc.), cedar, spruce and larch are primarily used. Of these lodgepole pine is probably the most common house log used in the custom home industry today. If we were to design a log home and had the option of all these different species, we would choose them accordingly. For the roof structure we would use Douglas fir because of its strength. The wall logs would be Western red cedar because of this tree's ability to resist decay and its high insulative value. We would then use lodgepole pine "character logs" for posting. "Character log" is a loose term used to describe wood that has natural figuring influenced by growth patterns of the tree. Many of these pine logs, while once cast aside as firewood, have become increasingly popular for posting, furniture, fireplace mantles, railings and other decorative work.

Along with a diversity of log species, comes various peeling techniques that can distinctly affect the overall appearance and feel of a home. While most full round log houses use clean peeled logs, others derive a more rustic look through "skip-peeling." This approach leaves some of the cambium layer attached to the log creating an irregular pattern of light and dark areas. Though the surfaces of these skip-peeled logs are, for the most part, smooth to the touch, they take on a highly textured appearance. Another option is to use weathered logs with some of their bark still intact. These logs also impart a rustic look and tend to make the building look old even when new.

Log End and Wall Profiles

Here is another area in which strong design elements prevail. While the profile of the logs within the walls (see *Illustration 21*) is important, it's the corners of the buildings that dictate, to a large degree, the overall style of the structure. There are many options from which to choose, and we have illustrated several of them here (see *Illustration 22*).

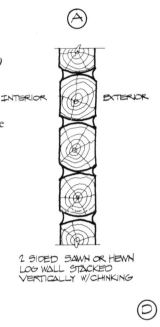
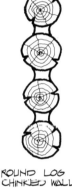
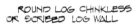

(A) (B) (C)

INTERIOR   EXTERIOR

2 SIDED SAWN OR HEWN
LOG WALL STACKED
VERTICALLY W/CHINKING

ROUND LOG
CHINKED WALL

ROUND LOG CHINKLESS
OR SCRIBED LOG WALL

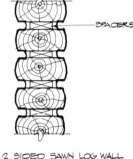

(D) (E)

SPACERS

2 SIDED LOG WALL
STACKED FLAT

2 SIDED SAWN LOG WALL
STACKED FLAT W/ SPACERS
& CHINKING

Illustration 21

Maintenance & Technical Notes   199

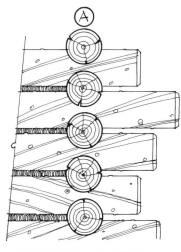

(A)

STAGGERED LOG ENDS

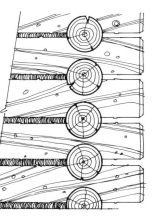

(B)

PLUMB LOG ENDS

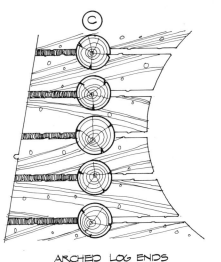

(C)

ARCHED LOG ENDS

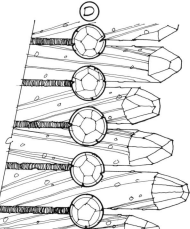

(D)

BEAVER CUT LOG ENDS

Illustration 22

Chinked Verses Scribed Log Construction

In the realm of log homes, there are two completely different building approaches. The first, which predominates in American logbuilding, is that of chinked construction, and it presents some advantages. Using seasoned material, the log work can proceed quickly, and the wood itself can be more irregular resulting in better log utilization. Electrical wiring is simplified because the wires can be hidden behind chink lines after the building has been erected.

Before the advent of the acrylic latex compounds, the chief drawback to the chinked style of building was the mortar itself. As pointed out in our discussion of this topic, the formulation of synthetic chinking compounds has eliminated problems that have plagued this building form for the past two hundred years. Ease of construction and traditional values have made chinked log homes the cornerstone of the hand crafted industry in the United States. In Canada, Europe and Japan however, a second chinkless or scribed log style prevails.

Logbuilding anchors its roots in scribed log construction, and there is one man who would not let this legacy slide into the mists of history. B. Allen Mackie of British Columbia, Canada has influenced the revival of traditional logbuilding like none other. His teachings have done more than just influence a whole generation of logbuilders—he created them. Exposure through his school in British Columbia, international workshops and his writings, have preached scribed log gospel to thousands of aspiring builders. He and his students have invented many different kinds of notches and developed innovative techniques for this method of construction.

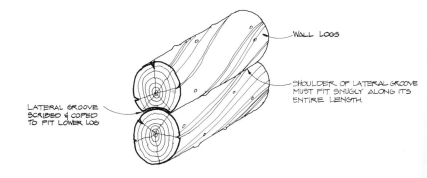

WALL LOGS

SHOULDER OF LATERAL GROOVE MUST FIT SNUGLY ALONG ITS ENTIRE LENGTH.

LATERAL GROOVE SCRIBED & COPED TO FIT LOWER LOG

SCRIBED OR CHINKLESS LOG JOINERY

Illustration 23

The appeal of the scribed log home is in its craftsmanship. All the logs must fit together perfectly. There is little room for error as the mated surfaces themselves provide a seal against the weather. This is both the strength and weakness of scribed log construction (see Illustration 23). A worker's skill and patience stands testimony to a perfectly scribed wall, where each log becomes a part of the log above and below. It's difficult to sustain this level of craftsmanship on the scale that is required by many log home companies to be competitive. The fact that so few of these buildings exist in the United States may be partly attributable to the direction set by the majority of home producers.

However, there are other building drawbacks that also play a role. One difficulty lies in keeping a well-scribed log home tight over time. Although builders well-versed in this construction go to great lengths to ensure that log shrinkage minimally affects the joints between the logs, it is difficult to maintain a complete seal throughout the life of the structure. This is especially true of homes built in dry climates such as the Intermountain West and southwestern parts of the United States.

One innovative approach to this problem has been tried by several builders with success. After the structure has been completed, but before windows and doors are installed, urethane foam is injected into the lateral grooves and notches. When this foam cures, it expands and forms a tight seal within. While effective, this procedure can be both expensive and messy. Since the foam is under a lot of pressure, it will tend to ooze from any gap between the logs. When fully cured, this excess foam is cut away, but residues can remain on the logs that will prevent acceptance of stains or preservatives. To avoid this, preservatives should be applied before foaming.

In conclusion, it is not our intent to pit one building style against the other. Particularly in less dry environments, scribed construction can be a very viable method of building. If you have your eye on an existing home with gaps and air infiltration, keep in mind that the exterior can be caulked or chinked without affecting the scribed look inside. Also, remember that when building with green logs, full scribed joinery must be used since log shrinkage will cause early failure of any chinking. So, if you admire this building style, by all means pursue it—just make sure you have a knowledgeable builder both on and off site.

Framing Considerations

Early log cabins were simple structures built entirely of logs. On the other hand, contemporary log homes, even those built to traditional designs, tend to use conventionally framed walls on the inside. There are many reasons for this including the lower cost of conventional framing, the need for electrical, plumbing and heating chases, and, perhaps most importantly, for interior design considerations. Many owners prefer some relief from logs.

Since conventionally framed walls will not shrink and settle with the logs, there are different framing guidelines for log homes. Most importantly, framing members must not impede log wall settling (see *Illustration 24*), nor should the connections between the framing members and the logs prevent this movement (see *Illustration 25*). Additionally, any drywall intersecting a log wall should be kerfed into the logs so that as the building settles and logs shrink away, gaps won't occur (see *Illustration 26*). Making the kerf slightly larger than the thickness of the dry wall will ensure that the logs can move past the material without binding. This gap can be filled later with paintable caulk to match wall color. Other areas of concern occur where logs meet glass and tile. Make sure that there is sufficient separation between these materials so that log movement will not create a problem.

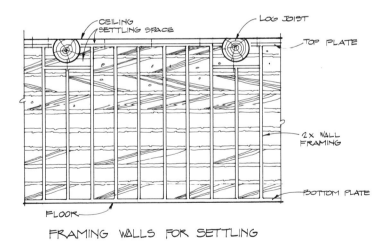

FRAMING WALLS FOR SETTLING

Illustration 24

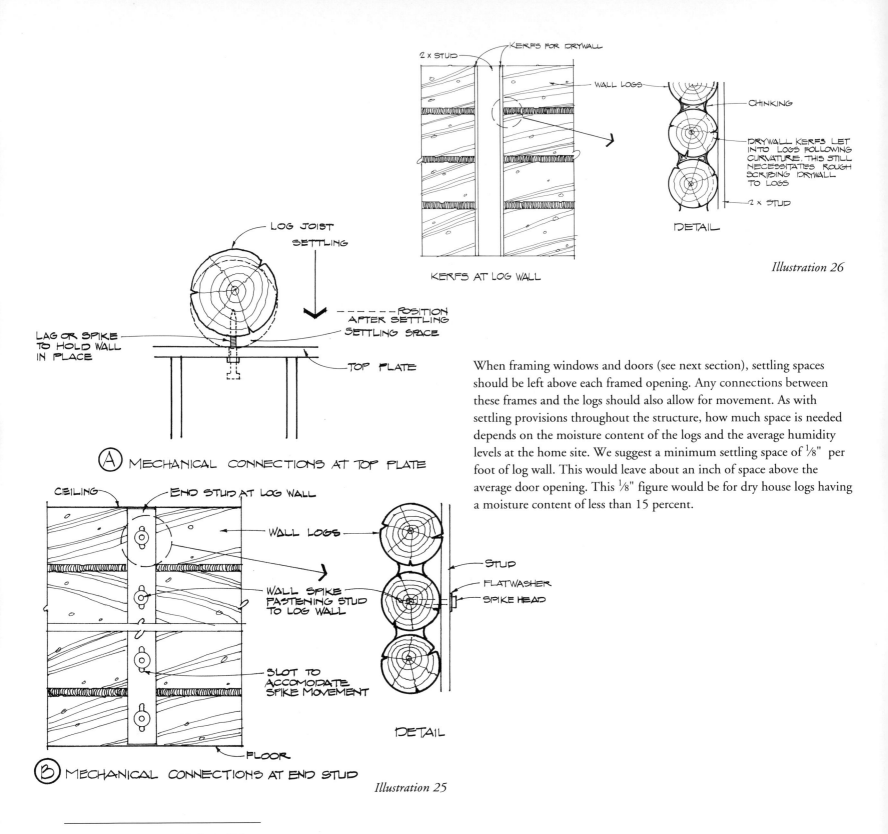

2 x STUD

KERFS FOR DRYWALL

WALL LOGS

CHINKING

DRYWALL KERFS LET INTO LOGS FOLLOWING CURVATURE. THIS STILL NECESSITATES ROUGH SCRIBING DRYWALL TO LOGS

2 x STUD

DETAIL

KERFS AT LOG WALL

Illustration 26

LOG JOIST

SETTLING

POSITION AFTER SETTLING

SETTLING SPACE

LAG OR SPIKE TO HOLD WALL IN PLACE

TOP PLATE

Ⓐ MECHANICAL CONNECTIONS AT TOP PLATE

When framing windows and doors (see next section), settling spaces should be left above each framed opening. Any connections between these frames and the logs should also allow for movement. As with settling provisions throughout the structure, how much space is needed depends on the moisture content of the logs and the average humidity levels at the home site. We suggest a minimum settling space of ⅛" per foot of log wall. This would leave about an inch of space above the average door opening. This ⅛" figure would be for dry house logs having a moisture content of less than 15 percent.

CEILING

END STUD AT LOG WALL

WALL LOGS

WALL SPIKE FASTENING STUD TO LOG WALL

SLOT TO ACCOMODATE SPIKE MOVEMENT

FLOOR

STUD

FLATWASHER

SPIKE HEAD

DETAIL

Ⓑ MECHANICAL CONNECTIONS AT END STUD

Illustration 25

Mechanical Hold Down Connections

There are a variety of hold-down connections *(see Illustrations 27)* for log walls. The one you choose depends, in part, on whether the logs are stacked directly on the foundation or laid up above the subfloor. Seismic conditions and local codes can also be a factor in design.

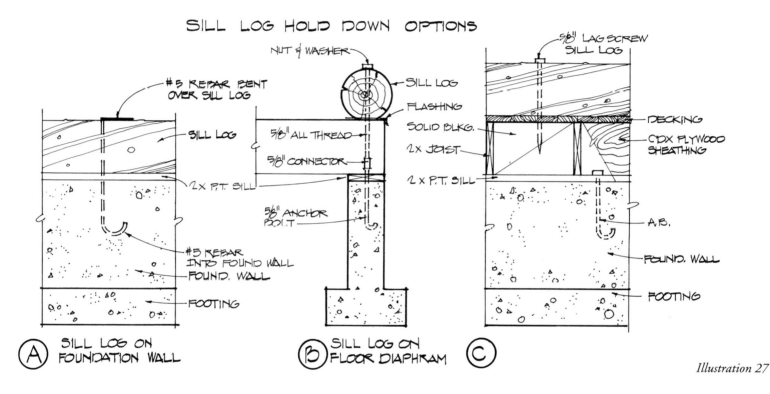

Illustration 27

Design and Implementation of Settling Devices

Mechanical settling devices can be as complicated as adjustable connectors or as simple as a wooden wedge (see *Illustration 28*). However, when using wedges or removable shims, make sure you have the ability to take the weight off the member when the time comes to make an adjustment. It does little good to have adjusting shims under a post that is too heavy to lift. It is also worthwhile to establish reference points around the structure so comparative settling measurements can be taken after the log work is finished (see *Illustration 29*). Without a benchmark from which to work, you are just groping in the dark.

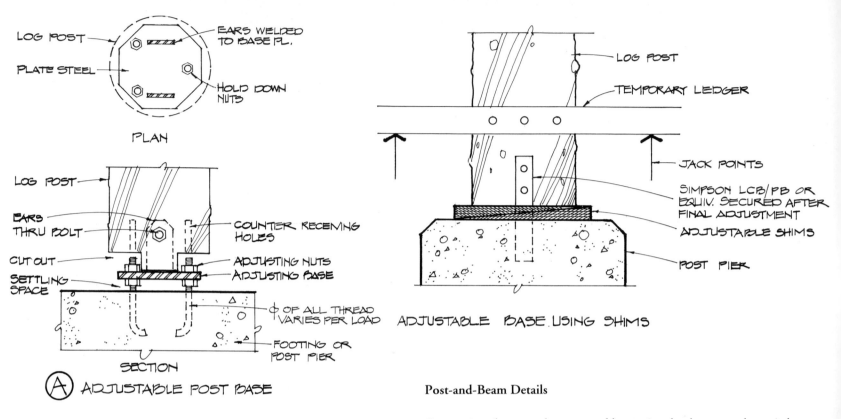

PLAN

Ⓐ ADJUSTABLE POST BASE

- LOG POST
- PLATE STEEL
- EARS WELDED TO BASE PL.
- HOLD DOWN NUTS

- LOG POST
- EARS THRU BOLT
- CUT OUT
- SETTLING SPACE
- COUNTER RECEIVING HOLES
- ADJUSTING NUTS
- ADJUSTING BASE
- Ø OF ALL THREAD VARIES PER LOAD
- FOOTING OR POST PIER

SECTION

- LOG POST
- TEMPORARY LEDGER
- JACK POINTS
- SIMPSON LCB/PB OR EQUIV. SECURED AFTER FINAL ADJUSTMENT
- ADJUSTABLE SHIMS
- POST PIER

ADJUSTABLE BASE USING SHIMS

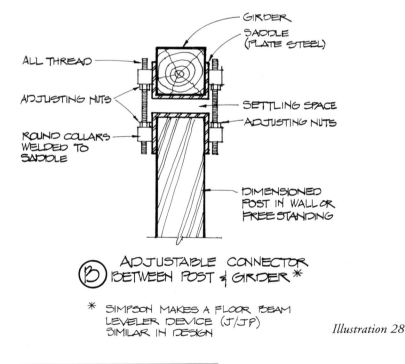

- GIRDER
- SADDLE (PLATE STEEL)
- ALL THREAD
- ADJUSTING NUTS
- SETTLING SPACE
- ADJUSTING NUTS
- ROUND COLLARS WELDED TO SADDLE
- DIMENSIONED POST IN WALL OR FREE STANDING

Ⓑ ADJUSTABLE CONNECTOR BETWEEN POST & GIRDER *

* SIMPSON MAKES A FLOOR BEAM LEVELER DEVICE (J/JP) SIMILAR IN DESIGN

Illustration 28

Post-and-Beam Details

Connections between the posts and beams in a log house can be varied and add much visual interest to the structure. Some of these connections are pictured here (see *Illustration 30*).

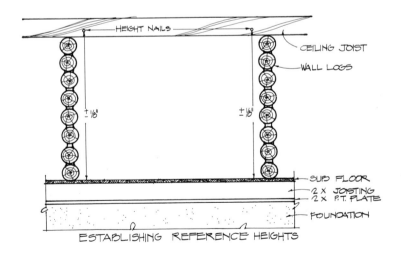

- HEIGHT NAILS
- CEILING JOIST
- WALL LOGS
- ± 1/8"
- ± 1/8"
- SUB FLOOR
- 2 × JOISTING
- 2 × P.T. PLATE
- FOUNDATION

ESTABLISHING REFERENCE HEIGHTS

Illustration 29

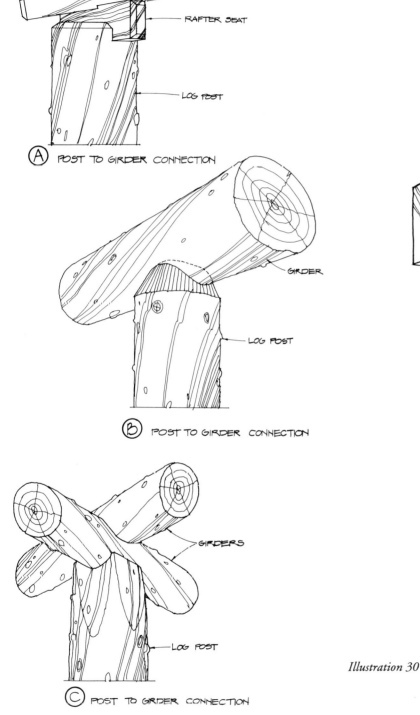

(A) POST TO GIRDER CONNECTION

(B) POST TO GIRDER CONNECTION

(C) POST TO GIRDER CONNECTION

Electrical and Plumbing Details

Previously, we noted how wiring can be hidden between the logs and covered with chinking. We also mentioned that framed walls will conceal electrical, plumbing and heating duct work. However, in the scribed log home, electrical wiring needs to be thought out a bit more carefully. In many cases, wiring needs to be run while the building is being erected. This is especially true for outside lights, receptacle boxes and switches. Otherwise, there is some opportunity to hide wiring behind door and window jambs. Installing electrical boxes in logs can be time consuming, and, when possible, it is best to install them in framed walls. Floor-mounted boxes can also be a time saver especially since wiring can be run through the crawl space.

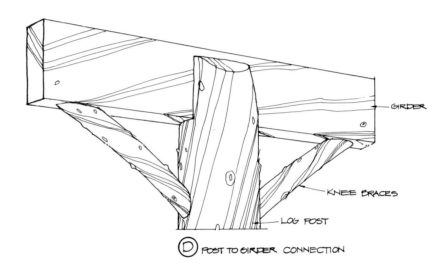

(D) POST TO GIRDER CONNECTION

Window and Door Framing Details

There are a variety of ways to frame windows and doors while accommodating most styles and designs. It would be impossible to cover every option here, so we will illustrate the most common.

Log or timber "bucks" can make a rugged and handsome frame-work around a window or door. They work well in a log house because of their scale. Good craftsmanship in this area can permit the rough framing members (bucks) to serve as finished jambs with the addition of stop material to complete the installation (see *Illustration 31*). The thickness of the buck material scales out best at three to six inches. This detail can also carry to the doors located in conventionally framed interior walls (see *Illustration 32*), though most times, it does not. There are drawbacks to this framing method including costs in terms of labor and materials.

Illustration 30

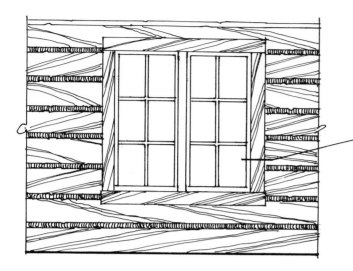

WINDOW IN LOG WALL

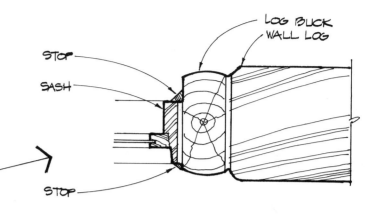

JAMB DETAIL

Illustration 31

Another option entails the use of two-inch framing material for rough or finished jambs, and there are several ways to go about this. One way would be to use material wide enough to cover the biggest log in the cutout. This may range anywhere from ten to fourteen inches on an average wall built with ten to twelve inch logs. The jamb could then be cased, inside and out, using more conventional trim materials such as 1x4, 1x6 etc. This presents a more finished look to the opening and may be important, if, for example, you are building to a particular design such as the "Craftsman Style."

A third option would consist of using 2x4 framing material to provide a nailing surface for the window flange (see *Illustration 33*). These doubled 2x4s would also serve as a base to fasten exterior and interior trim. The top piece of trim could be fastened to the header log and permitted to slip past the jamb allowing for log settling. Or this head casing could be fitted snugly, fastened with screws for easy removal, then taken off and trimmed later as conditions warranted. This method of window installation is very cost effective in terms of both labor and material.

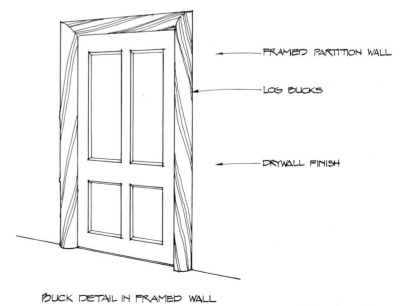

BUCK DETAIL IN FRAMED WALL

Illustration 32

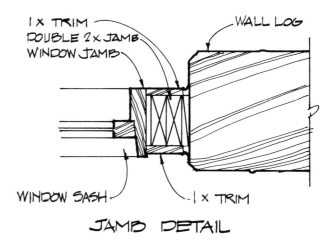

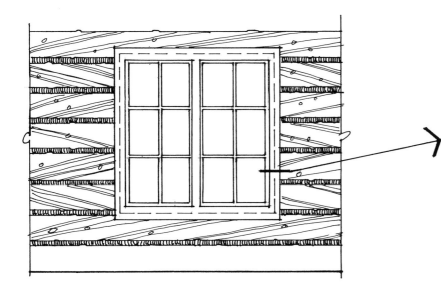

WINDOW INSTALLED USING
DBL. 2×4's AND FLANGE

Illustration 33

Finish Trim

Running trim on a log house can, and should, be a very creative process. It seems that no two houses trim out in the same way. From scribing in end panels of cabinetry, to providing slip joints between partition walls and ceilings, there are many challenges to face in this aspect of log home construction.

It would be ideal if the log work could season for a year or two before fitting the trim. Since this usually isn't possible, the builder must again take shrinkage and settling into consideration as this work progresses. A guiding principle is if trim work is run to log surfaces, then generally it needs to be "let" into the logs. This holds true for drywall, soffit material, base, casing or crown moldings. No matter how carefully this material is fitted to the logs initially, joints will open up as the wood shrinks.

MAINTENANCE & TECHNICAL NOTES BIBLIOGRAPHY

Articles

Fine Home Building. "Chinkless Log Building." Newtown, CT: Taunton Press, Inc., April/May 1989.

1993 Log Home Living Annual Buyers Guide. "Preventing Wood Decay," "Insects That Attack Wood," "Protecting Your Home," "Importance of Engineering," "Horizontal Log Surfaces," "Log Corner Intersections," "Log Sealing Systems," "Provisions for Log Settlement." Chantilly, VA: Home Buyer Publications Inc., 1993.

Muir's Original Log Home Guide For Builders and Buyers. "Log Home Construction and Maintenance: Preventing Decay and Insects," "How to Apply Chinking Properly," "The ABC's of Log Restoration." Crosby, TN: Muir Publishing Company Inc., Fall, 1988.

Muir's Original Log Home Guide For Builders And Buyers. "Log and Timber Trusses," "Preventing Air Infiltration in Roof Systems." Crosby, TN: Muir Publishing Company Inc., Fall, 1992.

Books

Goodall, Harrison and R. Friedman. *Log Structures— Preservation and Problem Solving.* Nashville, TN: American Association for State and Local History, 1980.

Mackie, B. Allen. *Building With Logs.* 6th ed. Prince George, B.C.:B. Allen Mackie and Ida Mary Mackie. P.O. Box 1205, Prince George, B.C. V2L 4V3, 1977.

Milne, F. Dan. *The Handbook of Canadian Log Building.* Quebec, Canada: Muir Publishing Company Limited, 1984.

Mitchell, James. *The Short Log and Timber Building Book.* Roberts, WA: Hartley and Marks, Publishers, 1984.

Phelps, Hermann. *The Craft of Log Building.* Ottowa, Ontario: Lee Valley Tools Ltd, 1982.

RESOURCE DIRECTORY

ORGANIZATIONS

Canadian Log Builders Association, International, 7928 Lynwood Dr., Ferndale, WA 98248, (206)354-5840

Great Lakes Logcrafters Association, 24411 Esquire Blvd., Forest Lake, MN 55025, (612)464-3843, Duane Sellman, (218)326-8627, Gary Schroeder

New Zealand Logbuilders Association, Rd. 2, Kopuaranga, Masterton, New Zealand, 06-372-5737, Angus McCallum

Rocky Mountain Logbuilders Association, P.O. Box 771253, Steamboat Springs, CO 80477, (303)879-3013, Paul Wellman

Timber Framers Guild, P.O. Box 1046, Keene, NH 03431, (603)357-1706

Association of Latvian Craft, c/o Ivars Strautins, Rozu-Iela 21-27, Riga, Latvia, LV-1056

Japan Log House Forum, c/o SELC CLB, 1-3-4-71, Minami-Cho, Kichijoji, Mushashino City, Tokyo, Japan 180, 0422-41-6659, 0422-49-5802 Fax

Korean Log Builders Association, Woorim Building, 90-10 Banpo-Dong, Seoul, South Korea, 02-463-2973

MAGAZINES AND BUILDER DIRECTORIES

Log Home Living. Home Buyer Publications Inc., 4451 Brookfield Corporate Dr., Suite 101, P.O. Box 220039, Chantilly, VA 22022. Bimonthly publication

Log Home Living Annual Buyer's Guide. Home Buyer Publications Inc., 4451 Brookfield Corporate Dr., Suite 101, P.O. Box 220039, Chantilly, VA 22022. Annual publication

Muir's Original Log Home Guide for Builders and Buyers. Muir Publishing Company Inc., 164 Middle Creek Rd., Cosby, TN 37722. Quarterly publication.

Muir's Original Log Home Guide for Builders and Buyers: Annual Directory. Muir Publishing Company Inc., 164 Middle Creek Rd., Cosby, TN 37722. Annual publication

Timber Frame Homes, Buyer's Guide. Home Buyer Publications Inc., 4451 Brookfield Corporate Dr., Suite 101, P.O. Box 220039, Chantilly, VA 22022. Bi-annual publication

Yume-Maru. Yama-To-Keikokusha Company Ltd./Sales Department. 1-1-33, Shiba-Daimon, Minato-Ku Tokyo 105 Japan. FAX: 81-3-5472-6290. Published three times a year. Full-color Japanese log home publication. Written in Japanese, but highly recommended

THE FEATURED HOMES AND THEIR CRAFTERS

ARCHITECTS, DESIGNERS, BUILDERS AND ARTISANS

It is impossible to list all current log home experts. Still, we present a partial list to aid interested home builders, buyers and decorators. We have met many of those listed here, and, in most cases, we have seen examples of their work. While confident that these individuals are competent, we don't represent them to be the most qualified in their field. Equally capable people may be found in your area. For a more complete list, consult publications listed in the Resource Directory.

Architects and Designers of Log Homes

Acker, Stan (Designer), P.O. Box 44, Ketchum, ID 83340, (208)726-8345

Architecture+, Stephen D. Pruitt, P.O. Box 208, Sun Valley, ID 83353, (208)726-3583

Berkus, Barry A. AIA, P.O. Box 1807, Sun Valley, ID 83353, (208)726-4228

Brown, Theodore, 1620 Montgomery St., Suite 320, San Francisco, CA 94111, (415)986-0101, Architecture and Interior Design

Clapet, William C. AIA, Architectural Associates, P.O. Box 1209, Crested Butte, CO 81224, (303)349-6188

Conger, Fuller Architects, 720 E. Durant St., Suite E-8, Aspen, CO 81611, (303)925-3021

Daley, John (Designer), P.O. Box 2949, Ketchum, ID 83340, (208)726-8678

Foote, Jonathan AIA, P.O. Box 25211, Jackson, WY 83001, (307)733-9021

Helland, Michael, P.O. Box 952, Crested Butte, CO 81224, (303)349-6583

Holmes, King & Associates, 575 N. Salina St., Syracuse, NY 13208, (315)476-8371

Jarvis, Janet AIA, P.O. Box 1183, Ketchum, ID 83340, (208)726-4031

Jerome, Gilbert, 152 W. 58th St., New York, NY 10019

Krantz, Richard John AIA, Richard Krantz Architecture, 1500 Quail St., Suite 520, Newport Beach, CA 92660, (714)752-6345

Lee, Vince, Design Associates Architects, P.O. Box 107, Wilson, WY 83014, (307)733-1261

Marvel, Jonathan H. AIA, P.O. Box 1602, Hailey, ID 83333, (208)788-2290

McLaughlin & Associates AIA, P.O. Box 479, Sun Valley, ID 83353, (208)726-9392

McMillen, Darryl AIA, P.O. Box 1058, Sun Valley, ID 83353, (208)622-4656

Munsterman, Dale, P.O. Box 625, Carnelian Bay, CA 96410, (916)546-3126

Nunn, Ellis & Associates, P.O. Box 7778, Jackson, WY 83001, (307)733-1779

Pries, Lynn, 18 Barristo, Irvine, CA 92705, (714)854-1785, Architecture and Interior Design

Ripsom, Peter, P.O. Box 885, Sun Valley, ID 83353, (208)622-8015

Ruscitto, Latham, Blanton, P.O. Box 419, Sun Valley, ID 83353, (208)726-5608

Schlechten, David A., AIA & Associates, P.O. Box 1027, Hamilton, MT 59840, (406)363-5641

Schmidt, H. Architects, 123 S. David, San Angelo, TX 76903-6396, (915)653-4242

Spence, LaNelle (Imaging), P.O. Box 548, Jackson, WY 83001 (307)733-8383, Designer and Interiors

Spitznagel Inc., Architects, 1112 W. Ave. N., Sioux Falls, SD 57104, (605)336-1160

Steinbrecher, Jean, P.O. Box 788, Langley, WA 98260, (206)221,0494

Tigerman, McCurry, 444 N. Wells, Chicago, IL 60610, (312)644-5880, Architecture and Interior Design

Zorn, Lee (Designer), P.O. Box 205, Free Union, VA 22940, (804)978-4785

Builders of Log Homes

A Very Unique Log Home, James Morton, Rt. 1, Box 2125, Roberts, MT 59070, (406)446-2406

Ackerman Hand Crafted Log Homes, Inc., P.O. Box 1318, Carbondale, CO 81623, (303)963-0119

Alpine Log Homes, Box 85, Victor, MT 59875, (406)642-3451

Appalachian Log Homes, 11312 Station West Dr., Knoxville, TN 37922, (615)966-6440

Ball, H. (General Contractor), Rt. 5, Box 276A, Charlottesville, VA 22901, (804)974-7400

Beamery, Inc., The, 620 Bull Run Valley, Heiskell, TN 37754, (615)947-3308, Timber frame homes

Beauchemin Construction (General Contractor), P.O. Box 1316, Jackson, WY 83001, (307)733-7640

Beaudet, Dean (General Contractor), P.O. Box 1745, Hailey, ID 83333, (208)788-9461

Black Bear Enterprises, Dale Clark, 8394 Kollath Rd., Verona, WI 53593, (608)832-4434

Brown, Wheelock, Crosby, Wheelock & Company, Rt. 1 Box 229, Washington, MO 63090, (314)239-5513, Architectural Consultants—Restoration Contractors

Canadian Handcrafters, Ltd., P.O. Box 364, Fernie, B.C., Canada V0B 1M0, (604)423-7932

Cascade Log Homes, P.O. Box 85, Kalama, WA 98625

Chambers, Robert Wood, Sparwood Homes, N8203 1130th St., River Falls, WI 54022, (715)425-1739

Clearwater Construction Company (General Contractor), Rt. 2, Box 4B, Rapid City, MI 49676, (616)331-6270

Ciulla, Robert (General Contractor), P.O. Box 64, Jackson, WY 83014, (307)733-1261

Custom Log Homes, Drawer 226, Stevensville, MT 59870, (406)777-5202

D & J Custom Log Homes, Rt. 3, Box 341, Zimmerman, MN 55398, (612)856-4600

Dave Carter Construction Company (General Contractor), P.O. Box 3360, Ketchum, ID 83340, (208)726-7555

de Alva, Bill (General Contractor), Final Touch Construction Company, P.O. Box 368, Telluride, CO 81435, (303)728-3670

Dembergh Construction, Inc. (General Contractor), P.O. Box 3006, Ketchum, ID 83340, (208)726-2440

Gelet, Alan H., Engelmann Inc. (General Contractor), P.O. Box 781, Ketchum, ID 83340, (208)726-9742

Golden Eagle Log Homes, Thomas Wood, P.O. Box 772418, Steamboat Springs, CO 80477, (303)879-3935

Gott, Peter, 155 Tater Gap Rd., Marshall, NC 28753, (704)656-2521

Gladics, John, P.O. Box 1379, Ketchum, ID 83340, (208)788-2029

Hearthstone, Inc., 1630 E. Hwy. 25/70, Dandridge, TN 37725, (615)397-9425

Highland Log Builders, P.O. Box 1750, Vernon, B.C., Canada V1T 8C3, (604)545-6655

Lakeshore Builders, Inc., (General Contractor), P.O. Box 5544, Tahoe City, CA 96145, (916)581-5544

Logcrafters, 17 James Ln., P.O. Box 1540, Pinedale, WY 82941, (307)367-2502

Logcrafters Log and Timber Homes, P.O. Box 448, St. Ignatius, MT 59865, (800)735-4425

Maple Island Log Homes, 10811 E. Hilltop Rd., Suttons Bay, MI 49682, (616)271-4042

Majestic Log Homes, Inc., P.O. Box 772 A, Fort Collins, CO 80522, (1-800)279-5646

McNamara Company (General Contractor), P.O. Box 1250, Sun Valley, ID 83353, (208)726-2372

McRaven, Charles, Charles McRaven Restorations, Drawer G, Free Union, VA 22940, (804)973-4859

Montana/Idaho Log Corporation, 995 S. U.S. Hwy. 93, Victor, MT 59875

Mountain Log Homes, P.O. Box 1128, Hamilton, MT 59840, (406)961-3222

Nash Construction, Inc., (General Contractor), P.O. Box 797, Ketchum, ID 83340, (208)726-4646

Oregon Log Home Company, P.O. Box 1377, Sisters, OR 97759, (503)549-9354

Original Log Homes, P.O. Box 1301, 100 Mile House, B.C., Canada V0K 2E0, (604)395-3868

Pioneer Builders, Mark Hankinson, P.O. Box 5176, Ketchum, ID 83340, (208)726-2683, Log building, restorations and rustic furniture

Pioneer Logs, Ltd., RR 2, Singhampton, Ontario, Canada N0C 1M0, (519)922-2836, Hewn log homes

Precision Craft Log Structures, 711 E. Broadway, Meridian, ID 83642, (208)887-1020, Precision milled log homes

Rath Construction (General Contractor), P.O. Box 874, Ketchum, ID 83340, (208)622-9322

Reed, James, P.O. Box 1024, Hailey, ID 83340, (208)788-2628

Riverbed Timber Framing Inc., P.O. Box 26, Blissfield, MI 49228, (517)486-4355

Rocky Mountain Log Homes, 1883 Hwy. 93 S. Hamilton, MT 59850, (406)363-5680, Offers custom and milled log homes

Rosen Log Homes, Inc., 1604 Airport Rd., Cloquet, MN 55720, (219)879-1888

Rustics of Lindbergh Lake, Inc., Star Rt. Box 2745, Condon, MT 59826, (406)754-2222

Sawtooth Construction, Inc., (General Contractor), P.O. Box 41, Ketchum, ID 83340, (208)726-9070

Spring Creek Timber Construction, Steve Cappellucci, P.O. Box 429, Almont, CO 81210, (303)641-3367

Stopol, Richard "Log Home," P.O. Box 1281, Hailey, ID 83333, (208)788-9693

Timberhouse Post & Beam, 150 Sheafman Creek Rd., Victor, MT 59875, (406)961-3276

Timberpeg Post and Beam, P.O. Box 474, West Lebanon, NH 03784, (603)298-8820

Torrance Construction (General Contractor), HCR1, Box 10, Lake Placid, NY 12946, (518)523-3225

Trans West (General Contractor), 4830 Rusina Rd., Suite C, Colorado Springs, CO 80907, (719)548-9522

Wildwood Log Homes, P.O. Box 1365, Pigeon Forge, TN 37868-1365, (615)428-1932, Custom-hewn, dovetail-notched homes

Wilkie, Jack (General Contractor), J Wilkie Builders, Inc., 0020 Sunset Dr., Suite 3, Basalt, CO 81621, (303)927-4226

Woody's Log Homes, Art Thiede, P.O. Box 3308, Ketchum, ID 83340, (208)788-4393, Building, restoration and maintenance of log homes

Interior Designers and Galleries

American West Gallery, Alan Edison, P.O. Box 3130, Ketchum, ID 83340, (208)726-1333, Offers cowboy and Indian antiques, folk art and collectibles and Molesworth and other vintage cowboy furniture

C. Boyer Designs, 8260 Lorain Rd., San Gabriel, CA 91775, (818)286-4111

Cortoy, Mary Ann, A. B. Closson Company, 401 Race St., Cincinnati, OH 45202, (513)891-5531

Dominick, Philae Interiors, 770 High St., Denver, CO 80218, (303)623-3800

Fagan, Bonnie, Design Concepts, 5807 32nd St. NW, Washington, DC 20015, (202)362-1183

Inner Design, 309 ABC Center, Aspen, CO 81611, (303)925-4310

Johnson, Paula G. Interiors, 8 Pine Rd., Colorado Springs, CO 80906, (719)635-5856

Lanham, Jacky, J. P. Lanham Designs, Inc., 472 E. Paces Ferry Rd., Atlanta, GA 30305, (404)364-0472

Lucini, Elizabeth Interiors, P.O. Box 3785, Ketchum, ID 83340, (208)726-8318

Manookian, Suzanne Interiors, Suzanne M. Inc., P.O. Box 2060, Sun Valley, ID 83353, (208)726-8516

Martin, Bruce Interiors, P.O. Box 2860, Ketchum, ID 83340, (208)726-5399

Niven, Susan Interiors, 901 N. Bundy Dr., Los Angeles, CA 90049, (310)476-3966

Pennino, Frank & Associates, 8654 Holloway Plaza Dr., Los Angeles, CA 90069, (310)657-8847

Riley, Kathleen Interiors, 2033 Claremont, Houston, TX 77019, (713)963-8315

Sagenkahn Designed Interiors, Chester Sagenkahn, 7189 E. Genesee St., Fayetteville, NY 13066, (315)637-1860

York, Sandra Interiors, 555 De Haro St., San Francisco, CA 94107, (415)863-9227

Young, Susan Interiors, 1000 Lenora, Suite 301, Seattle, WA 98121, (206)467-6869

Artisans and Furniture Makers

Adirondack Rustics, Barry and Darlene Gregson, Charley Hill Rd., P.O. Box 688, Schroon Lake, NY 12870, (518)532-9384, Birch bark, twig and contoured slat furniture

Beacon Woodcraft, Gary Dannels, "Twigologist," 307 Kilbourn, P.O. Box 11, Beacon, IA 52534, (515)673-6210

Bekan Rustic Furniture, Bud and Pat Hanzlick, P.O. Box 323, Belleville, KS 66935, (913)527-2427, Rustic tables, benches and chairs from Osage orange and recycled woods

Bryson, Kim, P.O. Box 2561, Hailey, ID 83333, (208)788-3648, Carved, solid-log furniture including beds, chairs, benches, night tables and bird houses

Burgess, Jack, Living Art & Design, P.O. Box 3271, Ketchum, ID 83340, (208)726-2566, Multi-media, woodcarver, sculptor, painter and furniture designer

Dodson, Lillian, 133 Crooked Hill Rd., Huntington, NY 11743, (516)427-2950, Contemporary, rustic, free-form, twig furniture

Elkhorn Industries, John and Sheri Bickner, P.O. Box 234, Jackson, WY 83001, (307)733-3916, Antler and horn furniture of the world (see p. 151)

Flynn, Gail, 3927 Oberlin Ct., Tucker, GA 30084, (404)491-0929, Antler artwork, interior design and rustic antiques

Great American Log Furniture Company, P.O. Box 3360, Ketchum, ID 83340, (1-800)624-5779, (208)726-8989, Sturdy pine furniture in styles ranging from rustic to refined contemporary

Greenwood Designs, Brad Greenwood, 13624 Idaho-Maryland Rd., Nevada City, CA 95959, (916)273-8183, Sophisticated rustic, twig furniture with a smooth, hand-sanded finish

Greg Adams Furniture, 914 E. Adams St., Muncie, IN 47305, (317)282-7158, Bent willow furniture

Hinds, Mark Swazo, P.O. Box 482, Tesuque, NM 87574, (505) 986-1626, Native American art including painting, sculpture and jewlry

Hink, Robb Craig, P.O. Box 3942, Ketchum, ID 83340, (208)788-5668, Whimsical cowboy wood art and furniture

Hunt, Liz, P.O. Box 218176, Columbus, OH 43221, (614)459-1551, Abstract, rustic furniture made by combining bentwood, stick and willow with other natural materials such as grapevines, nests and rocks

Jacques, Gibb, Box 791, Keene Valley, NY 12943, (518)576-9802, Birch bark and Adirondack, rustic furniture

Jones, Mary, The Chocolate Moose, P.O. Box 4162, Ketchum, ID 83340, (208)726-5256, Food art and gingerbread reproductions of your home . . . a big hit at Christmas time!

King, Don, HC67 Box 2079, Challis, ID 83226, (208)838-2449, Contemporary bentwood, rustic furniture, often incorporating colored and dyed woods

La Lune Collection, 930 E. Burleigh, Milwaukee, WI 53212, (414)263-5300, Willow and Amish furniture, steer hide rugs and pillows and other furnishings

Lemon, Jake (Woodworker), P.O. Box 2404, Sun Valley, ID 83353, (208)788-3004, Commissioned, one-of-a-kind, lodgepole pine furniture, often incorporating burls, rawhide and other rustic elements

Madsen, Matt, Burl Art Productions, P.O. Box 187, Orick, CA 95555, (707)488-3795, Rustic, free-form wood art combining roots and branches into functional furniture, distinctive clocks and phones

McAulay, Stephen, P.O. Box 363, Gaston, OR 97119, (503)359-1000, Hand-made willow furniture

McGregor, Brent, Rocky Mountain Timber Products, P.O. Box 1477 Sisters, OR 97759, (503)549-1322, Unique furniture created with ancient, twisted juniper, burls, antlers and other materials

Old Hickory Funiture Company, Inc., 403 S. Noble St., Shelbyville, IN 46176 1-800-232-2275, Hickory sapling frame furniture available in a variety of styles and finishes

Parish, Susan, 2898 Glascock, Oakland, CA 94601, (510)261-0353, Functional, sculpted art using driftwood and other "found" materials

Patrick, Mike J., New West/Patrick Ranch, 2119 Southfork, Cody, WY 82414, (307)587-2839, Traditional and contemporary western furnishings including Molesworth inspired designs using wood, wrought steel, leather, antlers, etc.

Robinson, David, 106 E. Delaware Ave., Pennington, NJ 80534, (609)737-8996, One-of-a-kind and limited editions—best known for rustic gazebos, gates, bridges, furnishings and garden architecture

Snyder, Susan, P.O. Box 2214, Ketchum, ID 83340, (208)726-5845, Painter, sculptor, see coffee table, page 73

Spence, Taylor, c/o Imaging Spence, P.O. Box 548, Jackson, WY 83001, (307)733-8383, Wall murals

Stark, Paul, P.O. Box 1381, Sisters, OR 97759, (503)549-0136, Wood sculptor

Sweet Water Ranch, Bryan H. Taggart, P.O. Drawer 398, Cody, WY 82414, (307)527-4044, Specializing in fine western furniture, accessories and Molesworth reproductions

Voisard, Micki, 999 Conn Valley Rd., St Helena, CA 94574, (707)963-8364, Innovative, handcarved, handpainted furniture, sculpture and accessories using the curving shapes of manzanita and madrone

Weisberg, Judd, Rt. 42, Lexington, NY 12452, (518)989-6583, Freshwater driftwood furniture

Log Home Building Suppliers, Masons and Metal Workers

Golay, Byrd, 3555 E. 4000 N., Kimberly, ID 83341, (208)423-5787, Stone and tile mason

Johnson, JL and Doris, P.O. Box 613, Bellevue, ID 83313, (203)788-9865, Chinking

Larew, Hugh, Rt. 5, Box 245, Waynesboro, VA 22980, (703)943-6417, Stone masonry

Pozzi of Idaho, P.O. Box 5130, Ketchum, ID 83340, (208)726-2345, A wide array of doors and windows, including Southwestern designs

Sheehan, Mark, P.O. Box 1815, Ketchum, ID 83340, (208)788-9475, Custom metal work

Summers, Sydney, P.O. Box 41, Red Cliff, CO 81649, (303)827-5881, Custom, handcrafted iron work

INDEX